(DIS)EMBODIED FORM

(DIS)EMBODIED FORM
ISSUES OF DISABLED WOMEN

Anita Ghai

SHAKTI BOOKS
An Imprint of Har-Anand Publications Pvt Ltd

HAR-ANAND PUBLICATIONS PVT LTD
E-49/3, Okhla Industrial Area, Phase-II, New Delhi-110020
Tel.: 41603490 Fax: 011-41708607
E-mail: haranand@rediffmail.com

Copyright © Anita Ghai, 2003
Reprint, 2006

All rights reserved. No part of this publication may be reproduced in any form without the prior written permission of the publishers.

Published by Ashok Gosain and Ashish Gosain for
Har-Anand Publications Pvt Ltd

Printed in India at S. D. Enterprises.

For my father...
who never saw my impairment as an obstacle, and whose faith and belief have enabled me to be who I am today.

Shakti Books Series

In a wide ranging and important new series, *Shakti Books* launches studies that provide thought provoking insights into how gender is inscribed in micropolitical practices across disciplines. Gender distinctions are necessarily located within a certain system of power structure. These distinctions are deliberately denied by that structure precisely because it valorizes the male. Conceiving gender as a field of experience which is socially constructed and constantly changing cultural practice, the series through investigative research, multiple data sources, and, media material, interrogate gender related issues from a variety of disciplinary and theoretical perspectives. It undertakes to sensitize readers to gender issues within the broader outline of an historically contextualized multidisciplinary criticism. Well known scholars from the field of social sciences to literary criticism; economics to politics critique topics such as desire, language, power, family, sexuality, representation, education and social structures to demonstrate the complex ways in which patriarchy succeeds in retaining its power in every sphere of life even in contemporary times.

Writings, using gender as a fundamental organising category of human experience, have appeared before but they remain scattered in books and journals. Moreover, little systematic attempt has been made to understand the close links of gender to traditional belief systems, social and cultural practices, colonial history and post colonial politics. *Shakti Books* makes these links and in a systematic way charts the field of overlapping and contradictory networks on gender to make it easily accessible to readers. Through its interventionary method, the series will make an important contribution to gender awareness in this country. What are the political implications of gender sensitization? How does this sensitization filter to the grassroot level? *Shakti Books* is the first series to consider and address some of these crucial questions in the context of both the national and the reigning transnational transactions in the world today. This challenging series offers more than a comprehensive introduction to modes of critical practice being used to trace the construction of gender in various disciplines.

TAISHA ABRAHAM
General Editor

Acknowledgements

First and foremost I would like to express my deep and sincere gratitude to Taisha Abraham for having implicit faith in me. Her patience and empathy, during the months after I lost my father, are hard to put in words. Had it not been for her constant encouragement at the personal level and her rigour as a General Editor, the book would have never seen the light of the day.

I also take this opportunity to thank Jesus & Mary College and the Department of Psychology, University of Delhi, for granting me study leave for a project that is an important part of this book.

On a more personal note, this book would have remained just an idea, had it not been for my friends and family. In particular, I am grateful to:

Vandana, for standing by me throughout this endeavour, both as a friend and editor. Her blunt and honest criticism helped me shape the book the way it stands today. Any lapses are my own!

Susan Gabel, Mairian Corker, Anita Silvers, and Alexa Schriempf, who kept sending me books and journals, but more importantly, provided the inner conviction that we, the disabled women, need to raise our voices. Dr. Mark Priestley, who initiated me into the 'exciting' area of disability studies.

Rachana who is always there. I don't even know where to begin to thank her.

My friend Praveen, though cynical about psychology and feminism but never skeptical about my abilities and work. His friendship made my days lighter.

Finally my family who has supported me unquestioningly and unconditionally in all that I have done. Words can never do justice to their contribution.

ANITA GHAI

Contents

Introduction   13

1. Understanding Disability   28

2. Disabled Women: Issues, Concerns and Voices from Within   56

3. Locating Disability in the Feminist Discourse: The Epistemic Contingency of the Disabled Feminists   91

4. Some Unresolved Issues   113

5. Moving Towards a More Inclusive Feminism: Re-thinking Disability   146

References   164

Index   177

Introduction

I have never encountered an image of a human body. Images of human bodies are images of men's bodies or women's bodies.

Moira Gatens, (1990, p. 82)

What will be your fate if your body isn't normal — and it has nothing to do with being fat or your ability to produce a son?

Srajana[1] (A disabled woman in India)

"To write is to struggle and resist, to write is to become, and to write is to draw a map" (Deleuze, 1992, p. 44). Deleuze's insightful statement is the cornerstone of my present endeavour to address the (Dis)embodied Form. My preliminary meeting with Taisha, my general editor, left me both excited and scared. For here was an opportunity to share my thoughts and experiences of a life marked with disability, with the academic community, and yet at the same time it meant opening myself up to a world which hitherto had ignored the realties of disabled women. Fearful, that I might cross the threshold of a discourse, where there may be no ready audience for my words, no clear listener, and the possibility that the voices of disabled women may not be heard, I asked Taisha for some time, and allowed myself to linger. I struggled to find a way of communicating my thoughts to intended readers without being banal. It was at this juncture that Foucault's article on 'technologies of self' came to my rescue (See Martin et.al. 1988, p. 9).[2] While responding to criticisms of his

---

[1] As an activist, I have come across a number of disabled girls and women. I share here some of their experiences. Needless to add that I am grateful to each one of them for permission to share their experiences as well as for enriching my own understanding of disability.

[2] As a practice, all feminist texts quote author's first names in the citations. Unfortunately, I have not been able to trace some first names.

problematization of the theoretical and epistemological classifications that govern the self, Foucault said, "The main interest in life is to become someone else you were not in the beginning. If you knew when you began a book what you would say at the end, do you think you would have the courage to write it?" While fully acknowledging the limits of my intellectual ability and comparability with his great mind, I found Foucault's voice reverberating in my head and pushing me to take on the present challenge.

Despite living and studying in apparently inclusive educational institutions, the intolerant attitudes of the Indian society towards disability always haunted me. Though I have continued to resist oppression by being both a part of the disability movement as well as women's movement in India, my reservations about sharing my lived reality with the outside world were very real.

The genesis of what follows reflects partly my own life experiences as a woman, who has contended with the existential realities of a visible physical disability. In this sense, it also records not only the pain and anguish of disabled lives, but also the resistance to the oppression inherent in living with a label which evokes and attaches a negative value to what it perceives as a 'lack' or 'deficit' as well as 'difference'[3]. The normative culture both in India and the world over, carries existential and aesthetic anxieties about difference of any kind be it caste, class, gender or disability. This is borne out by the people who have lived a peripheral existence on account of their deviation from the societal parameters that are considered normative leading to a creation of a living reality of acute marginalisation, discrimination and stigmatisation. My growing years were thus characterised by markers such as 'disabled', handicapped, crippled, differently-abled and special. The contradiction between the self and the other thus began very early in life as I began the process of contending with my disability and constantly comparing the appearance of my incomplete body with the perfect bodies surrounding me.

The internalisations that I carried in such a cultural milieu accustomed me to seeing my disability as a personal quest and tragedy to be borne alone. As a fellow disabled Ayesha Vernon puts it, "Social relations of domination shape our lives according to the number of privileges or penalties scored depending on the number of norms an

---

[3]Difference has been defined in innumerable ways. I use the term to signify a life condition that does not fit in with the norms of a given society, such as a deformed body.

individual conforms to or deviates from respectively" (Vernon, 1999, p. 389).

Though protected by a cohesive and supportive familial network, I learnt to cope with the limitations, imposed by my impairment. The recurring anxiety was to be ignored and relegated to the realm of what Freud so aptly termed as the 'unconscious'. My life in this way was what Frank calls a 'quest narrative' in which the introduction of disability was accepted and used to derive personal meaning. As Frank explains, "The genesis of the quest is some occasion requiring the person to be more than she has been, and the purpose is becoming one who has risen to the occasion" (Frank. 1995, p. 128). In such circumstances the most critical questions are asked, making it imperative to seek a meaningful existence. Coming to terms with the conflicting social imagery about disability and the realness of my condition, has thus been a long and lonely journey.

It was not too difficult for me to understand that socially, disability is represented as a deficiency that becomes the defining characteristic of the person and is accounted for mostly in terms of a medicalised biography. Constituted as being profoundly 'Other'[4] disability symbolically represents lack, tragic loss, dependency and abnormality. It is true that all of us begin life in a completely dependent state, often undergoing experiences of shame and loss. This comprehension however is moderated by the recognition that human minds and bodies are always in transition, moving from an incomplete, imperfect, and vulnerable existence to a relatively autonomous existence, (Winnicot, 1965). The possibility of this movement, however, is not accorded to the disabled, as it is believed that she/he does not have to deal with the vulnerabilities or lack, unlike the whole person who has to come to terms with it and therefore suffers more. There is thus a refusal by the able-bodied society to recognise that the impaired human being is different but not deficient. In recent years, though there has been a lot of attention devoted to the body along the axes of class, caste, gender

---

[4] I use the 'Other' to refer to a process in which an individual or society attempts to convey a label such as disabled, dalit or woman. As Bill Hughes and Kevin Paterson say (1997, p. 325), "The response to impairment in modernity has been essentially anthropoemic: disabled people have been cast in the role of other and cast out: imprisoned by what Foucault (1967) called the 'great confinement' and excluded from and denied access to many of the key sites of power and privilege". I deal with the process of othering with the help of Memmi's work in the next chapter.

and sexuality, any reference to the disabled body has been severely lacking. For most disabled people, (including myself) ignorance displayed by the social world colours our identity formation. Whether we, who are designated as 'different' do not see ourselves as 'dalit', poor, crippled, or disabled, these terms nevertheless describe an essential reality in a society tuned to the tyranny of normality and perfection.

Very few people accept the fact that disability is as much a social construct as other categories such as gender. In short, disability is conceived as a naturalised category. Society thus exhibits a structural amnesia about a particular category of people, who, because they do not fit into the hegemonic discourse of 'normality', are excluded, separated and socially dis-empowered. This social and cultural apartheid, is sustained by the existence of a built environment which lacks amenities for the disabled and solely caters to the needs of the more complete and able-bodied 'Other'. This social disregard coupled with experiences of social, economic and political subjugation deny the disabled a voice, a space, and even power, to disrupt these deeply entrenched normative ideals that deprive them their social presence and any semblance of identity. Disabled people, especially women are encouraged to be childlike and apologetic towards the able-bodied society, which judges them as the beings that would have been better dead than alive (John Swain and Sally French, 2000).

To survive as a disabled person in such a blinkered social environment has meant coming to terms with unequal power relationships. This is reflected most clearly by an absence and invisibility in the most forward-looking social movements and dialogues in India including the women's movement. Such disregard results in an ignoring of pertinent issues with regard to disability from the point of view of both active social struggle as well as contemporary academic discourse. Unfortunately such incipient stigmatisation against those who carry the insidious label of 'disability' with them results in an exclusion that creates both a sense of despair and distress, often leading to a suppression and non- recognition of the 'lack' that marks them initially as different.

Perhaps it is reflective of such socialization that despite an attack of polio at the age of two, for over three decades I refused to recognise my own limitations caused by my disability. With a body that was/is socially stigmatised as 'the Other' and labelled as disabled, my dilemma, like that of others like me, had been about whether to situate myself as a 'positive mind' or a 'negative body' in a largely unfriendly social environment. It was not till I was in my early thirties, that a certain objectivity entered my world view and I began questioning my condition and that of others like me and the social responses to it. Exhibiting, I believe, a severe form of denial, I initially refused to acknowledge the processes which labelled me as disabled and sought to stamp me with a definite identity. Though conscious of the public eye and the confusion, which would often result as I transgressed many of the limits that society imposed on my 'kind', I continued to be an active, independent, and mobile individual unlike the expected social norm.

However, neither my consciousness nor my self proclaimed standing as a feminist gave me the courage to carry the basic assertion of the personal being political, over to my disabled existence. As a psychologist, my research queries incorporated the dimension of disability, though, I never dared to debate with the societal formulations about the inner world of disabled people, specially disabled women. Instead as an active participant in the disability movement,[5] my main objective became developing awareness and creating sensitivity in the mainstream society regarding disability issues so that the hegemony of the abled could be challenged and contested by the disabled.

Having spent the last five years actively fighting for the realisation of rights of the disabled, I have realised that disability is not the only social marker of distinctiveness as gender coalesces with it and makes the experience doubly oppressive. Most of the fights for the rights of the disabled both in the developing countries, as well as the developed world, are male-centric. Within the Indian scenario, the bias gets reflected in the primary questions raised by the disability movement in the past decade. The concerns have been related to issues such as employment, inclusion in the census, implementation of the disability legislation and more recently accessibility to the built environment. The very fact that, in India, it was a visit from Stephen Hawking that

---

[5]The disability movement got initiated with the declaration of year 1981, as the International year of disabled people (IYDP). Till then, sporadic attempts had been made to rehabilitate the disabled. It was after 14 years of struggle, that legislation saw the light of the day.

underscored the complete inaccessibility of the built environment, for both the public and the government is a sad commentary on the disability movement's vision of the fight in which it is engaged.

Regarding issues concerning women, the disability movement in India has not fought a single battle which has focussed on feminine concerns such as reproductive health and the violence of basic rights against disabled women.[6] For instance, the widespread case of forced hysterectomies in government as well as private institutions all over the country do not elicit any reaction from the leaders of the disability movement who are essentially middle class elite men. Instances such as these indicate that disabled women are simply not regarded as women. Their silence is only reflective of the general social malaise and the patriarchal tradition that locates women in passive roles. Within such institutions there are also indications of sexual abuse towards female residents. Renu Singh, an activist (Personal Communication) reports incidents of male staff members fondling female resident's breasts each time they bathed them. Verbal abuses are also prevalent, such as "you are a burden to society" and "your parents should have killed you". Even in the day care centres women often hear the staff hurling abuse such as "one who can't wipe her own shit has no right to be concerned about her hair, let me chop off your damn hair" (Ghai forthcoming).

The situation in the west[7] is not significantly different which is clear from a statement by Michelle Fine & Adrienne Ash who say, "Having a disability presumably eclipses these dimensions of social experience. Even sensitive students of disability...have focused on disability as a unitary concept and have taken it to be not merely the 'master' status, but apparently the exclusive status for disabled people" (Fine and Asch 1988, p. 3).

Feminists with disabilities all over the world have complained about the male domination and male orientation of the disability movement, which makes many feminists with disabilities uneasy members of the

---

[6]It is possible that some individual women have benefited from the efforts of various women's groups. My contention is that the issue never received any focused attention.

[7]In chapter three, I share the viewpoints emerging from the epistemic contingency of disabled women, who have contributed in fighting for a space for disability within feminism.

disability rights movements. Israel and McPherson (1983, p. 20), state this precisely when they describe how "Disabled feminists...feel uncomfortable in the disability movement because it is often male dominated and at times blatantly sexist". That the scenario has not changed much is evident from Carol Thomas's detailed analysis and conclusion that, "The experience of disability is always gendered, that disablism is inseparably interwoven with sexism (and racism, and homophobia, and so on). This is not to say that disabled women and men have no common ground, no shared experiences of disablism, but that the forms of disablism are always refracted in some way through the prism of gendered locations and gender relations" (Thomas 1999, p. 28).

Like the west, the struggles of the disabled in India too, have ignored the impact of gender. More painful however is the neglect of disabled women by the feminist discourse in India. Different social movements in India, spearheaded by women, have attempted to question and fight patriarchal oppression. As Kamla Bhasin and Nighat Said Khan state, "Feminism is an awareness of women's oppression and exploitation in society, at work and within the family, and conscious attention by women and men to change this situation... a struggle for the achievement of women's equality, dignity and freedom of choice to control our lives and bodies within and outside the home... for a just and equable society for women and men both" (Bhasin and Khan 1986, p. 3).

The above sentiments do not, however, include the lives of disabled women, who thus feel marginalized by their own fraternity, otherwise a natural ally. By failing to pay attention to disability as a life condition, feminists whose theory presumes to include disabled women under the general rubric of 'woman' fail to recognize the different experiences of disabled women in a sexist and able society. Interestingly, even in the west the neglect has been felt acutely. However feminists who have either become disabled as a result of a chronic illness, or, acquired disabilities at a young age did take up the related issues. These scholars have to some extent redeemed the situation; the feminist discourse in India however continues to exclude the concerns of disabled women (Anita Ghai, 2002c, p. 56).

Consequently women, continuously appear as secondary partners, in a male-centric and ablest hegemony. It is true though that disabled women, in general, do not deal with the same oppressions that non-disabled women do primarily because disabled women are not seen as women in an able-bodied society. For example, women with disabilities have not been 'ensnared' by many of the social expectations that feminists have challenged. However, this confinement is actually indicative of a negative rendering of their lives as the usual roles such as marriage and motherhood are out of bounds for them. While it is true that the specific issues for women with disabilities may vary from those of non-disabled women, the reality of womanhood which includes the usual experiences and fears of a patriarchal society are bound to be similar. However, with a body that does not 'measure up' to societal norm, the situation becomes precariously unbalanced.

One reason for this has been that within feminist discourse, the challenging of the universal subject of 'woman' was problematised only recently. In the Indian scenario, the calls for inclusion were often met by a patronizing tokenism, which argued that though exclusion of disability was real, the system was helpless to challenge the perfectionist norms of a biased society. The helplessness stems in part from too many issues to be confronted, a resource crunch, and possibly the anxieties associated with body disintegration. Those who debated over public policy did not feel the need to include the issue of disability within their purview. Despite attempts by activists to include the issue of disabled women in the agenda of a national conference on public policy in Hyderabad in January 2000, the organisers expressed their inability on the pretext that there were more pressing concerns to be discussed. Couched in politically correct language, the message of course was clear that the disabled women do not count as significant.

For Indian feminists, disability continues to be used almost synonymously with the identity of being a 'woman' such that its specific character does not receive its due and is lost in the concern/ lack of concern for women's rights in general. It is true that in a country like India, where there are innumerable problematic issues, some prioritisation does take place. However, for the disabled women the resulting scenario becomes a replication of the patriarchal order where the male order decides on what the agenda and priorities of human life should be. Consequently, assumptions are made about a hierarchy of oppression and disabled women do not find any space in this hierarchy. Their concern is limited and myopic, which results in paying only lip service to the demands made for inclusivity. Recently at a public seminar, a leading feminist told me to read Kaleidoscope (an American publication on disability), to satisfy my desire to understand the issues pertaining to the lives of disabled women in India. My intention is not to negate the significance of sensitive magazines such as Kaleidoscope, which do a wonderful job of creating awareness about the lives that get labelled as disabled. I quote the above to contextualise the location of Indian feminism vis-a-vis disabled women and to share the irony of the situation, where one has to turn towards an American publication to understand the position of disabled women in India. The suggestion in my view is not reflective of a stance that wishes to engage with the issue of disability—so much for the rhetoric of inclusion. My experiences with the academy have left me more bewildered and have also reinforced the assertion of many disabled people, both women/and men, that disability is perpetuated when it is associated only with the experiential terrain without any meaningful connection with critical thinking about feminism or culture.

Once again, I must reiterate that disabled women in the western world have not had it easy either. In fact it was the engagement with difference, which began in earnest in the western feminist discourse especially since the second wave of feminism, that led to the recognition of impaired and disabled bodies. It took a long time to draw attention to the masculine bias of the disability theory, and to criticise the exclusion of disabled women from the feminist theory. (See Susan Wendell, 1996; Helen Meekosha, 1990; Jenny Morris, 1996; Carol Thomas, 1999). Various strands within western feminism as a political movement taking its vantage point from the world of women's experience began to acknowledge the universal nature of the problem, and by default the exclusion of those living at the periphery and margins. Yet as very eloquently put by Elizabeth Weed, "For those outside mainstream feminism, women's experience has never ceased to be problematic. The common ground of sisterhood long held as white feminism's ideal was always a more utopian than representative slogan. Worse, it was coercive in its unacknowledged universalism, its unrecognised exclusions" (Weed, 1989, p. xxiv).

It was in this exclusion that the disabled women have had more than their fair share. If at all, the gender dimension has been considered, it has been through a 'double disadvantage' hypothesis. The feminist discourse in the west attempted to connect disability theory and feminism by arguing that disabled women must deal with the twofold but separate oppressions of being a woman in a sexist society and being disabled in an ablest society. Once each oppression has been charted out, one can then 'add' the two together to understand the disabled women's oppression. In other words a disabled women faces dual oppressions, one on the level of 'disability', the other on the level of 'gender'. Both the identities are similar in that they are both social constructions derived from two biological facts—one of impairment, the other of sex. Moreover as Alexa Schriempf says "both identities are similar in that neither impairment nor sex in and of themselves are problematic or difficult—that is, they become a problem only when placed in a social context that is designed to be unwelcoming to those biological characteristics" (Schriempf 2001, p. 65). So, if the reality of disabled women's lives is to be comprehended, the negativity associated with both sex and impairment needs to be visualised. Further their interaction in formulating 'dual oppression' for disabled women has to be understood. Many feminist thinkers in the field of disability have objected to this double disadvantage, as such writings, they believe, do not empower. Morris, shares her discomfort about the rendering of disabled women's lives in writers such as Susan Lonsdale (1990, p. 208) who write about disabled women in terms of compound and unique kinds of oppression. Says Jenny Morris, "I feel burdened... I feel a victim... such writings do not empower me. We have to find a way of making our experiences visible, sharing them with each other, and with non-disabled people, in a way that—while drawing attention to the difficulties in our lives—does not undermine our wish to assert our self worth" (Morris, 1996, p. 2).

An 'additive' framework in which the attempt is to understand separate oppressions and then add them back together as if that would explain the whole experience marks this kind of thinking. An implicit assumption of this model is that gender, disability, impairment, and sex are binaries. As a result, disabled women are theorised about by adding the two "biological foundations" of sex and impairment together to conclude that disabled women are oppressed along the twin axes of gender and disability. The approach very clearly rests on biological foundationalism, suggested by Linda Nicholson (Nicholson, 1995, p. 42). According to her, biological foundationalism has enabled many feminists to retain the idea of biological determinism that the constancies of nature are responsible for certain social inadequacies. From the feminist perspective, this demands the acceptance of the position that such social constancies cannot be transformed. However, what is problematic is that such uncontested notions always have a bearing on human subjectivity (Ibid, 2).

Notwithstanding these critical issues, theorising of difference has continued to neglect disability. In the words of, Helen Meekosha "The normal mind cannot encompass a difference so profoundly embedded in its/our sense of the 'normal' and its silenced Others (those who are not the part of the taken-for-granted everyday world of the dominant cultures)" (Meekosha 1998, p. 161).

When the popular metaphor posits women as being inherently disabled, as it does in India, it forecloses the possibilities of a meaningful dialogue of the category that is being used as a symbol. Consequently the emancipatory possibilities are lost, as attention is focused on the main object, which is women in this case, leading to the marginalisation of the disabled voices, which for cultural reasons have anyway never been heard. It would perhaps be wiser to recall Trinh Minh-ha's caution, "Theory is no longer theoretical when it loses sight of its own conditional nature, takes no risks in speculation and circulates as a form of administrative inquisition. Theory oppresses when it wills or perpetuates existing power relations, when it presents itself as a means to exert authority—the voice of knowledge" (Trinh Minh-ha, 1989, p. 42).

This book is thus a critical engagement with the void—both social and political—that I have experienced within my world of reality as a disabled woman academic and an activist in a traditionally patriarchal society. Recent estimates indicate that there are roughly 35 million women who are disabled in India. (Ali Baquer and Anjali Sharma 1997). That the women's movement chooses to ignore this marginalized section is evident in the complete absence of the issue from every platform they address, be it academic discourse or active struggle. For instance, the status reports brought out by the apex bodies such as the National Women's Commission testify that disability is not an issue which attracts the feminists. In most of the feminist transcripts, many of which I could quote, disability is conspicuous by its absence thereby remaining an undefined entity who, in this reading, have no cultural standing. Even Kali a publishing house, committed to the cause of the women, has not come forth with any meaningful engagement with disability.

The feminists' fight against oppression in India is not really concerned with disability as an issue is clear. Perhaps they are waiting for disabled women to raise their own voices. While this might be a just expectation it ignoress the social, economic, communication as well as architectural barriers, that disallow disabled women from sharing their stories and engaging in a public discourse.

I hope the present endeavour will underscore the reality that for the Indian feminist—to borrow Jane Flax's terminology—"the model person in feminist theory still appears to be a self sufficient individual adult" (Flax, 1987, p. 640). The disabled female is to be excluded because of an unwillingness to explore the constitution of gender relations, in contexts of experiences of living in a culture, in which bodily perfection is a central organizing principle of society. I do trust that the book will manage to address the concern of disabled women within the Indian context, and expand the definition of what feminism means to them, while making feminists re-think categories that need to be incorporated.

While my attempt is that the book will resonate with the lives of disabled women, I cannot be over ambitious, as any attempt to represent the experiences of all women with disabilities, is going to raise questions about the possibility of authentic representations of those disabled women for whom disability might be just one of the markers of oppression. As I have written elsewhere (Ghai, 2002a, p. 89), disability both for men and women in the Indian context is not a singular marker. It has to be situated in multiple contexts which comprise of other markers of difference and inequality such as poverty, caste, class and religion.

Consequently, even though the vantage point for me is the innumerable stories and voices of many women who have a range of disabilities, the lens through which they have been understood and presented is obviously mine. I am bound to shift back and forth between my own location as a researcher on disability issues with a background of psychology, and as an activist with the disability movement and as a disabled person myself.

Such a work can only be a miniscule interjection in the debate on the reality of disability. An interjection, because, the struggle against the hegemony of normality and patriarchy, with which I and others like me have grown up, is an ongoing one. In this sense it is also a testimony of a life that I have lived, both as an academician and as disabled woman. The reader will thus come across both the experiential terrain as well as the theoretical nuances, which have situated that experience.

The book is divided into five chapters. The first chapter gives a brief background of disability theory. Disability has been a contested term, defined in different ways. While some definitions follow a purely medicalised approach, activists all over the world have pressed for the recognition of its social character. What therefore constitutes disability, is a question that is not easily answered. The western world continues to engage in debates that ponder over the meanings and the nuances of the terminology that is utilised in the discussions of disability. Although, the disabled people's movement in India started somewhere in the early eighties, the development of disability studies as an academic endeavour is still to be recognised as a legitimate field of study. Consequently, while there have been attempts by scholars and activists such as Anima Sen (1988) and Baquer and Sharma (1997), these works read more as status reports, rather than serious academic inquiries. Gareth Williams' contention that, "The language of disability has become the object of political analysis, and it is becoming increasingly difficult to use terms to describe chronic illness and disability innocently" (1996, p. 194), does not hold much weight in India. Within the scope of this chapter I highlight the tricky issues involved in the categorisation of disability. I have attempted here to locate gender as a special issue in the male-centric disability theory.

The second chapter deals with the issues, voices and concerns of disabled women in India. In a cultural scenario, where the birth of sons is privileged, being born a disabled girl can be considered a fate worse than death. While I have given a bird's eye view regarding disabled girl's experiences, I have also included some voices that speak about their lives in and outside their immediate family and community through the use of personal narratives. To a feminist mind erasures of any group appear problematic. While the neglect can be bemoaned, a more constructive exercise is to analyse the reasons for the exclusion. I have made an attempt to highlight the reasons both within the Indian scenario as well as the developed world. In my understanding, the exclusion experienced by the disabled women is a direct consequence of the process of 'Othering' that they have to go through. Since disability provokes fears and anxieties about one's own mortality, it very easily renders itself as the 'Other'. The process of 'alterity'[8] needs to be understood to comprehend the experience of exclusion.

In chapter three, the focus is on some of the theoretical viewpoints that have emerged from the epistemic contingency of the disabled feminists. The idea is to share with the readers the discourse that has emerged in the process of negotiation of both disability as well as feminism. While one attempt is to highlight the kind of work that has been undertaken by the disabled feminists, the chapter is intended to underpin some of the key issues neglected in both the feminist as well as the male stream disability discourse.

Chapter four addresses in detail some of above issues. From the vantage point of a feminist, the explanations of disability as pure social constructions are problematic as they overlook the material body. The ramification of an essentialist perspective on body vis-à-vis the social constructive position has to be understood in order to comprehend the site where disability is produced. In the existing disability theory, two different positions are discussed. While one views 'disability identity' as a social construction, the other sees disability as conceptually distinct from impairment. This distinction becomes even more critical when the attempt is to link both the disability theory and the feminist discourses. The chapter thus endeavours to map out the different strands that are significant in raising these issues. Further it also looks at the ramifications of following 'identity politics' and its nuances. Within the feminist discourse the need to understand the nuances of engagement with 'difference' is critical. While a hierarchy of oppression can be established, the question is about its efficacy in resolving the crisis of lives that are oppressed. The reader will find that I offer no single answer, as my attempt is to engage more with the

---

[8]The idea of alterity has its origin in Hegel's dialectic. According to Bill Hughes (2000) alterity animates the biomedical distinction between the normal and the pathological. This is embedded in Edward Said's work, *Orientalism* which I discuss in chapter two.

tensions that need to be sensed in order to evolve a more inclusive theory and practice.

Finally, I look at the spaces where a feminist discourse can take the issues of disabled women forward. I do that with a hope that even though universal sisterhood is problematic, feminism still has the potentiality of aligning itself with the disability movement in a quest for resisting the hegemonic discourse and, locating the 'agency' that can struggle against the 'naturalised selves' that society creates for those women, who carry the label of being broken bodies.

The book, I hope, can address disability as a societal phenomena, thereby representing more than a subjective personal experience. As a fellow disability activist Simi Linton states, "Disabled people, across the broadest spectrum of disability, have solidified as a group. Although this group identity has certainly not been comfortably embraced by all disabled people, a strong disability alliance has led to civil right victories and the foundation of a clearly identified disabled community. The cultural narrative of this community incorporates a fair share of adversity and struggle, but is also, and significantly, an account of a world negotiated from the vantage point of the atypical. Although the dominant culture describes that atypical experience as deficit and loss, the disabled community's narrative recounts it in more complex ways. The material that bind us is the art of finding one another, of identifying and naming disability in a world reluctant to discuss it and of unearthing historically and culturally significant material that relates to our experience" (Linton, 1998, p. 5).

1

Understanding Disability

Emancipatory research is about the systematic demystification of the structure and processes which create disability, and the establishment of a workable dialogue between the research community and disabled people in order to facilitate the latter's empowerment.

Colin Barnes (1992, p. 122)

The goal of any academic discourse is to develop an understanding which can articulate the everyday 'living reality' of the constituency that it is concerned with. Within the field of disability, this has been done through developing models of disability. Though the term model has been used in a number of different ways, its use in disability research is that they represent a particular type of theory, namely structural which seeks to explain phenomena by reference to an abstract system and mechanism (Llewellyn and Hogan, 2000, p.157). Theories in all such discourses are based on a certain set of assumptions about the nature of reality or knowledge. The reality however, that gets defined by a disability theory may or may not hold uniformly for every disabled person. Consequently, a thought provoking analysis of such theories that purport to explain disability must be undertaken for it is imperative to understand the nuances of the concept which gets defined as 'disability'. An engagement with the definitions and terminology utilised in disability discourse is absolutely essential. "Who is disabled?" is a query, which to date is a highly problematic one because any reflection on the construction and use of the term signifies its pervasiveness beyond what can be taken as its normative bodily marker. For a feminist project this becomes even more problematic, as feminists are committed to the idea of altering/ changing women's lives. They are thus watchful in ensuring that the theories and terms by which any discourse develops does not remain an isolated and exclusive hierarchical body of knowledge constituting what Meaghan Morris (1995, p. 50), refers to as a 'peculiar doxa' that constitutes a single-minded, ponderous and phallocentric conversation.

To delve deeper into the notion of 'who is disabled?' one has to understand the different strands within which the understanding of disability has been gained and comprehend the finer shades of the terms and definitions that determine the fate of those labelled as 'disabled'. Though there are innumerable definitions of disability, Michael Oliver and Colin Barnes (1998, p.14), suggest that definitions of disability can be divided into two groups: official definitions produced by professionals and academics; and those developed by disabled people and organisations controlled and run by them. The definitions of disability assume significance as they are instrumental in diagnosing a particular condition as belonging to a specific category which can have far reaching consequences in shaping the identity of those subjected to its ramifications. Diagnosis, can be understood, both as a medical process as well as a system of analysis of people's lives based on special knowledge and expertise of professionals. It is a tacit agreement within particular disciplinary areas to make sense of certain events in a certain way.

Kenneth Gergen et al. suggest that, "diagnoses, official and unofficial, often concretise identities that limit people; they create black boxes with few obscure exits, and they form obstacles to more viable and liberating definitions" (1996, p. 5). On the other hand Sutcliffe and Simons suggest that, "The acquisition of a label can open gates to resources and other forms of support that are not generally available" (1993, p. 23). In this sense the diagnostic label is like a double-edge sword. Unless you have it you don't get access to services. However, once you have it, labels can be instrumental in the exclusion of some people from the mainstream society. A feminist engagement with the discourse of disability has to reflect a concern with the diagnostic systems, which give a sense of legitimacy, confidence and predictability both to the professional and to the client. It is only within the purview of feminism that certain questions can be articulated. For instance, who has the power to name? Who seeks diagnosis and why? How reliable are diagnostic systems? What part does diagnosis play in the maintenance of professional power? What role does diagnosis play in creating potentials and restricting possibilities for disabled women? As diagnosis is intrinsically connected to the definitions of life conditions labelled as disease/disability/impairment, it is important to understand how these terms get defined.

Within the Indian context, I have chosen to highlight three definitions of disability and terms that are often used synonymously. The first one is a definition given by World Health Organisation (WHO) which intervened in the arena of disability by introducing a threefold scheme known as International Classification of Impairments, Disabilities and Handicaps, popularly known as ICIDH (WHO, 1980). The threefold division categorises impairment, disability and handicap separately. This has been by far the most popular definition that has decided the fate of millions of disabled individuals.

International Classification of Impairments, Disabilities and Handicaps (ICIDH) (WHO, 1980[1]):

Impairment: In the context of health experience, an impairment is any loss or abnormality of psychological, physiological or anatomical structure or function.

Disability: In the context of health experience, a disability is any restriction or lack (resulting from an impairment) of ability to perform an activity in the manner or within the range considered normal for a human being.

Handicap: A disadvantage for a given individual, resulting from an impairment or disability that limits or prevents the fulfilment of a role (depending on age, sex, social and cultural factors) for that individual.

The second significant source of definition in the last few years within the Indian context is provided by the Indian legislation entitled "Persons with Disabilities Act" (Equal opportunities, protection of rights and full participation) passed by the Government of India in 1995. The Act uses the broad category of people with disabilities and under its rubric, puts the areas of functional limitation without really questioning the boundary lines which decide the difference between normal and diseased. The fact that limitations have a social and cultural meaning is not reflected in these definitions. I have taken a

[1] In year 2001, WHO introduced a new classification scheme. However, since most of the discussions continue to operate in terms of the older scheme, I have not included the 2001 classification as part of the definitions.

few illustrations to demonstrate how these definitions seal the fate of the person who comes under their ambit.

Definitions given by the "Persons with Disabilities Act" (Equal Opportunities, Protection of Rights and Full Participation):
1. Blind: A condition when a person suffers total absence of sight;
2. Visual acuity not exceeding 6/60 or 20/200 snellen (in the better eyes with correcting lenses);
3. Limitation of the field of vision subtending an angle of 20 degrees or worse;
4. Cerebral Palsy means a group of non-progressive conditions of a person characterized by abnormal motor control posture resulting from brain insult or injuries occurring in the prenatal or infant period of development;
5. Hearing Impairment means loss of sixty decibels or more in the better ear in the conversational range of frequencies;
6. Leprosy Cured person means any person who is cured of leprosy but is suffering from loss of sensation in hands or feet as well as loss of sensation and paresis in the eye.

Strangely enough, definitions given by both WHO as well as the more recent Indian Legislation do not reflect definitions propounded by the disabled people themselves. As early as 1976, the Union of the Physically Impaired against Segregation (UPIAS), expressed a need for an alternative definition of disability. In its manifesto document, it clearly implicated society as responsible for disabling impaired people. It thus gave a definitional scheme, which is as follows.

Defintions of Impairment and Disability: Union of the Physically Impaired Against Segregation:

Impairment: lacking part or all of a limb, or having a defective limb, organism or mechanism of the body.

Disability: the disadvantage or restriction of activity caused by a contemporary social organisation which takes little or no account of people who have physical impairments, and thus excludes them from the mainstream of social activities.

As must be evident to the readers, the definitional riddles in disability are extremely significant as they decide the fate of the person designated as disabled. However, whether it is WHÓ, Indian Legislation or the activists themselves, the disabled people acutely feel the ramifications of the definitions. My own understanding is that disability is not really a fixed category most clearly signified by the white cane user or a crutch user. Rather it denotes a fluid and shifting set of conditions. As Mairian Corker points out, "Disability, like most dimensions of experience is polysemic—that is ambiguous and unstable in meaning— as well as a mixture of truth and fiction that depends on *who says what, to whom, when and where"* (Corker, 1999, p. 3) (the emphasis is mine). Many categories such as muscular dystrophy and myalgic encephalomyelitis are not as fixed as perhaps the polio is. Even polio changes its character as is evident from the development of post polio syndrome in young polio survivors as they become older.

Within the Indian legislative framework, the identity of disability is thus contingent on the certification process carried out by the state constituted boards which inadvertently work on the basis of the degree of impairment. To be defined as a disabled, a certification of 40% impairment or more should be there. Some state benefits such as a discount in air travel are given to visually impaired and to the mobility impaired who have 80% or more disability. What is critical for a feminist account is the recognition that these assessments all over the world become what Maragrit Shildrick and Janet Price (1996) call the 'Foucauldian exercises in disciplinary power'. The feminist world can perhaps recall these issues in connection with rape cases such as that of Bhanwari Devi in Rajasthan.[2]

The sentiment reverberates in the lives of disabled women both in India as well as rest of the world, as they do not visualise how these individual, medical classification are helpful in comprehending their experience.

Another consequence of these classifications leading to labelling is that once they become fixed categories, they are never really re-examined. For instance, once a medical certificate is given, reassessment

---

[2]For a detatiled analysis of this case see Taisha Abraham "The Politics of Patriarchy and *Sathin* Bhanwari's Rape" in *Women and the Politics of Violence* ed. by Taisha Abraham (New Delhi: Shakti Books, 2002), pp. 277-291.

of the disability is never done. Moreover there is no uniformity in the assessments as a wide discrepancy is noticed in the certificates obtained from different states or different hospitals within the same state. As mentioned earlier, the fact that there might be appreciable change in given conditions such as muscular dystrophy or polio is therefore not reflected in the definitional closures inherent in a one time certification process.

Notwithstanding, these anomalies, disabled people in India were excluded from the census of 2001, on the basis of the figures obtained from the census of 1991. The rationalisation for this decision was that the 1991 census revealed a very low incidence, which did not warrant the creation of this category in the census 2001. What was omitted from the discourse was that the 1991 census framing of disability was in terms of a total incapacitation. However, no individual, despite the severity of the impairment is or can be totally incapacitated. The reality that Kargil[3], the cyclone in Orissa[4] and more recently the riots in Gujrat are adding up to the seventy million disabled people in India is often overlooked.

It is in this context where even a head count is seen as seemingly redundant, that the issue of disability has to be understood. The reluctance clearly indicates that disability is not conceived as a social rights issue or as a developmental issue which marginalises a certain class of people, but remains an invisible and inconceivable life condition. This is despite the fact that no one is more than temporarily able bodied.[5] Susan Sontag's discussion of illness as metaphor illustrates this stance. For her, "Everyone who is born holds dual citizenship in the kingdom of well and in the kingdom of sick. Although we prefer to use only the good passport, sooner or later each of us is obliged, at least for a spell, to identify ourselves as citizens of that other place" (Sontag, 1979, p. 3). The attempt on Sontag's part is to separate the essential from the non-essential aspects of illness, and by inference, disability. Sontag's objective is to liberate our thinking from

---

[3]Though, the exact numbers are not known, Kargil, a confrontation between India and Pakistan has been responsible for adding on to the population of 70 million disabled in India.

[4]A report by NDTV indicated the plight of the disabled in the aftermath of the super cyclone in Orissa.

[5]TAB is an acronym used by the disability community to refer to what they consider "Temporarily able bodied".

the "punitive or sentimental fantasies" concocted about illness (Ibid, p. 3). Kriegel, in a discussion of Sontag's work, notes that "disease has become so all-embracing a metaphor that its actual consequences have been swallowed up by the welter of moralistic judgements it calls forth" (Kriegel, 1982, p.17). However, both these observations are not made in the context of disabled people who live out the consequences of these metaphors. Thus disabled people are often granted permanent citizenship to the kingdom of sick by a society that categorises disabled persons as the 'Other'. Lackmund (1998), reminds us, "As constructionist perspectives in the social studies of science suggest, diagnosis are not merely neutral means for the transmission of knowledge. Instead they are actively involved in the very production of the phenomena they represent" (Lackmund, 1998, p. 780).

Whether congenital or acquired later in life, disability, results in consequences, which include marginalisation, in every sphere of life. Whether it is denial of education, employment, recreation, income, identity or social recognition, the overall impact on the mental health of the affected person is definitely negative. In living with disability, people try to make sense of their experience in the light of the systems of meaning and practices that are provided by the culture in which they reside. Within India, disability is often understood culturally as a retribution for past sins. The disabled are stigmatised as having a deficient personality and the emphasis is on medical cure as far as possible. The social, economic and political aspects of disability become secondary. The medical response thus remains the overarching social response to disability. Within the disability discourse this response has been read as the medical interpretation of disability, thereby creating what is now known as the individual/medical model of disability. Before proceeding further, it is important to understand the medical model.

The Medical Model of Disability

The medical model makes two fundamental assumptions. Firstly, it locates the problem of disability within the individual. Secondly, it seeks the causes of the problem as stemming from the functional or psychological limitations that arise from the individual disability. The scientific, objective and humane exterior of the medical model has not been able to hide the fact that, within its practices, there lurks a considerable ambivalence towards the people it professes to aid. Cure and overcoming of the disability thus become the overarching themes of the medical perspective. Since the pathology is located in the individual, the responsibility of procuring the cure lies with the person who is afflicted with the disability. However, cure in the Indian scenario where resources are meagre, and numbers innumerable, is extremely difficult to offer. While the philosophy of care and rehabilitation has enhanced the reputation of the medical profession, the disabled people continue to receive the implicit message that they are deficient and abnormal. If they have to become "valued" persons, then they would have to overcome their disabilities.

Rehabilitation professionals adopt practices which are aimed at improving the "quality of life" by making a person "function" better. It is realised that while functioning might improve certain aspects of life, the ultimate quality of life, is contingent on a sense of positive identity. However, the emphasis that rehabilitation professionals place on functioning leads many disabled people to consider their own bodies as enemies and declare a war on them. Consequently, the therapeutic focus overrides a sense of fun and play, with play becoming recreational therapy, art being transformed to art therapy, and, music and theatre, taking the role of drama therapy. Every activity is construed as a way to making the disabled 'better' and supports the premise that they are not good enough, adequate and normal. Rehabilitation is thus inextricably linked with oppression and a direct result of social and cultural commitment to 'normalcy' as a kind of 'perfection' where normal standards of ability, appearance, and behaviour are the criteria for what is allowable: if you don't measure up, you are inferior.

Even within medical sociology, which supports a social model of health, disability is often reduced to invalidism. It uses the notion of the invalid, or sick person as one who is incapable of undertaking any social responsibilities and as dependent upon the care of others. For instance, the licences given to disabled drivers who drive automatised vehicles still label them as drivers of invalid carriages. Further, a request for a wheel chair while booking an air ticket carries the label of the person being invalid. As Simi Linton argues, "some disabilities do result in weakening of the body, or, more likely, parts of the body, but the totalising noun invalid, does not confine the weakness to the specific bodily functions; it is more encompassing" (1998, p. 28).

Colin Barnes and Geof Mercer say, "medical sociology has tended to investigate all impairments ... from an illness perspective. Disabled people are both defined and confined by medical jurisdiction" (1996, p. 5). Their inability to deal with their disabilities is a rationalisation for keeping them out of sight—whether in an institution or in a private home. The model thus locates the problems as stemming from the bodies of disabled people, leaving little scope for negotiating the bias and discrimination experienced by them. The stress on the medical condition coupled with a total disregard for societal intervention institutionalises oppression and discrimination.

This understanding reduces the identities of the disabled to medical categories, thereby limiting their scope for social and cultural participation. Segregation in mainstream education, employment, difficulties in public transport and absence from the labour market, become markers of this disabled identity. Traditional psychology has replicated this model by use of tools such as Intelligence Quotient (IQ) tests and the mental health measures. Both are riddled with disablist, sexist, and middle class values. Much of psychology has not enriched the quality of life of disabled people. On the contrary it continues to reify intrinsically social and economic problems within communities as individual medical anomalies requiring clinical treatment, rather than socio-political intervention. Psychology thus continues to play a significant role in giving labels to people with a total neglect of context that is responsible for the label.

Far from being beneficial, or even neutral, the medical and psychological constructions have been at the core of creating the notion of disability, as very profoundly the 'Other'. Confinement through inability enunciates, at a cultural level, the medical and social policy response to disability. In actuality the constructions themselves are debilitating, but medicine has seen them as the solution to disability, rather than as a process that is constitutive of it. Furthermore, the very notion of incapacity, in the medical vocabulary, not only assumes a biological dysfunction, but places this dysfunction as the root cause of disability. The position, clearly absolves social arrangements from both causation of and responsibility for disability.

To make matters worse these medical considerations are always underpinned by what has been described as the personal tragedy theory of disability (Oliver, 1990), which suggests that disability is some terrible chance event which occurs at random to unfortunate individuals (which in India is attributed to past sins as mentioned earlier). The discourse asserts both implicitly and explicitly that disability is a personal tragedy, thereby becoming the root cause of the most intrusive, violating and invalidating experiences that the disabled go through in the medical field. The tragedy, as mentioned earlier, is to be avoided, eradicated and normalised by all possible means. This applies both to the disabled person as well as the familial world to which she/he belongs.

The personal tragedy model posits a "better dead than disabled" approach and reinforces the stereotype that the disabled cannot be happy or enjoy an adequate quality of life. The disabled person's problems are perceived to result from bodily impairment and a troubled mind, rather than the failure of society to meet that person's needs in terms of appropriate human help and accessibility. This understanding places specific burdens on the disabled to reconstruct themselves as normal people as they contend with both implicit as well as explicit assumptions about their reluctance to acknowledge their disabled existence. Consequently, disabled people are subjected to many disabling expectations by the able-bodied society. For it is mandatory for them to be 'independent', 'normal', and to 'adjust' and 'accept' their situation. Very often, the unrealistic expectations cause more damage to the sense of self of the disabled person than the impairment itself. Oliver sums up this view with his observation that, "The individual model for me encompassed a whole range of issues and was underpinned by what I called the personal tragedy theory of disability. But it also included psychological and medical aspects of disability .... In short, for me, there is no such thing as the medical model of disability, there is instead, an individual model of disability of which medicalisation is one significant component" (Oliver, 1996a, p. 31).

The medical focus within the Indian context is clearly evident from the Indian human development report, which states that, "physical disabilities are genetic, biological and even birth defects and future research must focus on the causes of such disabilities" (Abusaleh Shariff, 1999, p. 148), thus, reiterating that medical intervention is regarded as a prerequisite, without any contemplation of the social perspective. It too locates disability as inherent to the disabled person and consequently his/her personal tragedy.

The tragedy model of disability personifies at one level a fear of death, and can be read as an attempt to deny the inevitability of death. An alternative account, however, suggests that the tragedy perspective has a rational, cognitive basis constructed through experiences in a disabling social context (Swain and French, 2000, p. 573). Basic to comprehending a non-disabled person's tragedy view of disability is the possibility of crossing the gulf between the binary of disability and ability. It is true that the non-disabled are 'TABs' or 'temporarily able bodied'. Consequently, unlike the split between the people of different genders or different races, non-disabled people daily experience the possibility of becoming impaired and thus disabled. As Irving Zola argues, "any person reading the words on this page is at best momentarily able bodied, but nearly everyone reading them will, at some point, suffer from one or more chronic diseases and be disabled, temporarily or permanently, for a significant part of their lives" (Irving Zola, 1982, p. 242).

Thus, the fears are not so 'irrational', as the underlying cause has a very strong rational base. However, the fears definitely operate at the level of the unconscious, because if the non-disabled people were fully conscious of the uncertainty, the attitude towards disability would have been different. On the contrary, this causal link becomes intrinsic to the tragedy model. To become orthopaedically impaired, for instance, will be a personal tragedy for a someone whose life is based on mobility and who lacks knowledge of the experiences of people with mobility impairments. For such a person, self-identity is founded on being able to walk. For him/her the inability to walk would definitely imply a personal catastrophe and thoroughly devastating experience. The observation of the very real difficulties that the disabled have in education, work and relationships compounds the feeling of disaster. Such harsh realities create a further divide between the disabled and the non-disabled, particularly through the association of disability with dependence and abnormality. To be non-disabled means that one has been able to avoid the tragedy of disability and is thus not the unfortunate one.

The problem, however, is that the tragedy model of disability and impairment is often internalised by the disabled people. The oppression that stems from a multitude of stigmatising factors appears to have a rational basis, which explains why it is so difficult to question the tendency to self blame and guilt that the disabled carry with them. Living through a daily onslaught of professionals, experts, family and media invalidating their disability experience, the expression of resistance is likely to be interpreted as unrealistic. It will, on the contrary, be constructed as lack of acceptance, unnecessary bravery, compensation or simply ignored. Non-recognition of the oppressive structures of society and rights of disabled people accentuates the problems experienced by the disabled. Similarly, for a non-disabled person whose life is constructed on the basis of being normal, the impairment is experienced as a tragedy, perhaps augmented by the trauma of illness or accident.

Thus, the medical model with its clear interpretation of disability as a personal tragedy encourages the disabled to 'rise above' and transcend the body. Whatever the difficulties, they are expected to be borne by overcoming them. Discouraged to pay attention to whatever aches and pains that might be experienced, the disabled are expected to go about their lives as though their bodies are immaterial. Indeed, it is because the body is held in such contempt that we are able to find ourselves living in a world that is structured, as Susan Wendell has pointed out, "as though everyone can work and play at a pace that is not compatible with any kind of illness or pain" (Wendell, 1997, p. 39).

In this manner, disability becomes either totally invisible or as suggested by Mitchell, hyper-visible (Mitchell, 2001, p. 393). The latter which might be understood as being remarked upon, noticed or stared at, can be understood if it is placed in some relation to its dialectical twin: invisibility. The most pertinent example is Ralph Ellison's novel, *Invisible Man* (1952), which explores the dynamics of exchange and transformation between the invisible and the visible. Ellison's invisible man is not literally invisible. His problem is that his racial markings as an African-American are hyper-visible, and so his identity as a human being and speaking subject is rendered invisible. This sort of permissibility and invisibility that derives from it, are certainly critical to the experience of disability. This is very similar to what Iris Marion Young (1990) calls the paradoxical oppression, where the marginalised group is made invisible through cultural norms that set it up as the

'Other', and simultaneously marked out as different by stereotypes (Young, 1990, p.58). The experience of cultural imperialism means to experience how the dominant meanings of a society render the particular perspective of one's group invisible at the same time as they stereotype one's group and mark it out as the Other. In the Indian context stereotypical labels such as *Langri* (cripple), *surdas* (blind), and *mand buddhi* (mentally retarded) send a message of dependence and passivity, condemning individuals to repeat narratives of a constant struggle to fight the negative images associated with the labels.

Consequently, those who dare to call attention to their bodily "imperfections" are shunned. Their demonstrated inability or refusal to "rise above" the body is taken as evidence of their inferiority, and they are not taken seriously.

Aesthetic Model of Disability

Another way of conceptualising disability is provided by Susan Gabel, who puts forward an aesthetic theory of disability. According to her, the development of one's 'embodied self' through the process of experiencing life is significantly influenced by personal interpretations which are unique to each disabled person. The disabled body interacts within a social environment but 'identity itself starts with the body: what the body does, how the body looks, what the body says, how the body feels, and how others experience that body" (Gabel, 1998, p. 12).

In developing a theory of an aesthetic of disability, Gabel elaborates further, "When I say 'I am disabled', I say something about the culture within which I experience life, its values, its norms. I also consider my disabledness in light of my other body experiences (gender, ethnicity, race, sexual orientation) and how those are constructed and valued or de-valued in culture. Finally, if my statement appears to disagree with the prevailing notions of my culture, then my claim is one of resistance to those notions, and, in the end, my claim collaborates with my culture to construct my disabled body. In the end, my statement says much about me and how I view my body and my self but it also says much about the others with whom I experienced my world" (*Ibid*, pp. 74-75).

Gabel's viewpoint can, therefore, be understood as conceiving disability in terms of multi-dimensional experiences that use background factors to construct meanings of cultural identity. However, this understanding springs from within a mind/body consciousness that has the capacity to resist and transform values about disability, as well as the capacity to reject notions imposed externally. In other words, that statement, 'I am disabled' may be influenced by mainstream cultural ethos, but is eminently a conscious personal choice. Claiming one's own disability signifies identifying with a disability community and treating it as an aesthetic pursuit. It is an act of decoding in which this aesthetic pursuit creates a cultural identity within which experiences takes on a more positive and altered meaning. This is in close correspondence with Harlan Hahn's argument that the disabled people, need to reclaim/reconstruct an aesthetic tradition by deconstructing images of the body as a gestalt or whole body image. Instead of the whole, separate and discreet parts of the body need to be emphasized. In place of a gestalt we need to 'cultivate a heightened aesthetic appreciation of anatomical variations' (Hahn, 1988, p. 223). As Susan Peters says, "This view requires that one rejects conformist visions of beauty and assert that disability is beautiful" (Peters, 2000, p. 596).

The last decade thus has witnessed an increased awareness about the issues related to disability. Activists throughout the world have fought against the essentialist medical identity and negative cultural constructions associated with it. The consequent emergence of the disabled peoples' movement highlighted the inadequacy of individualistic psychologies and necessitated the development of broader social approaches.

While the medical model demands that disabled people adapt to society, the alternative model which has been termed as the 'social model' demands changes in the social structures so that needs of the disabled can be reflected. An insight into the social model is required to understand the need for a shift away from the medical/tragedy model of disability.

The Social Model of Disability

The social model challenges the assumption that both problems and solutions lie within disabled people rather than with society. The model arose as a protest against the medical model of disability, which treated disability and impairment synonymously so that disability was located within the body or mind of the individual, whilst the power to define, control and treat disabled people rested within the medical and paramedical profession (Oliver, 1996a). A major proponent of this model emphasised that the problem of disability is to be located within society. The cause of the problem is thus not the individual limitations, of whichever kind, but the society's failure to include the needs of the disabled people in its social organisation. The model was borne out of the experiences of disabled people, challenging the dominant individual models espoused by non-disabled people who fail to accept that the disabling factor is not the wheel chair user, but the built environment which has zero accessibility. Historically, it was when activists challenged these conditions that, the Union of Physically Impaired against Segregation (UPIAS) redefined disability and made a clear distinction between the concepts of impairment and disability. Thus while impairment is concerned with the biological "lacking part or all of a limb, or having a defective limb organism or mechanism of the body", disability is seen as social: "the disadvantage or restriction of activity caused by a contemporary social organisation which takes no or little account of people who have physical impairments and thus excludes them from participation in the mainstream of social activities" (UPIAS, 1976, p. 14).

This definition was broadened to include all impairments. This interpretation challenges the ideological hegemony of the medical model. It emphasises that disability is not an illness like measles. In this sense while impairment might be an individual attribute, disability is described as "the outcome of an oppressive relationship between people with impairments and the rest of the society" (Vic Finkelstein, 1980, p. 47). Negative attitudes, limited physical access, limited access to communication and resources, are considered as impediments that interfere with the disabled individuals to actualise his/her potential in the desired roles. The model thus focuses on disability as a diversity of human condition and not as an undesirable trait to be fixed or cured. This approach, unlike the medical approach, analyses the experience of illness and disease in the context of the social factors that are indeed responsible for producing and perpetuating disability. The genesis of this model lies in the analysis of materialist history advanced by Oliver.

Oliver posits that disability is related to economic and social structures and to the central values of modes of production. He adds that the individualised and medical approach to disability is attributed to the functional needs of a capitalistic society which requires able-bodied people who are physically and intellectually fit. Barnes et.al (1999) while elaborating on the theory have indicated that it is not simply the mode of production, but rather the mode of thought and its connectedness with the mode of production (Barnes et. al, 1999, p. 84). According to them the serious economic changes brought by capitalism affected the social relations with overarching implications for family life. Coupled with the population growth, these factors threatened the given social order. According to Oliver (1990), the development of capitalism, results in disability taking a specific form (the personal tragedy model) and the social oppressions become more acute. Consequently, the institution becomes the major controlling factor. For Oliver, the institution embodies both repressive and ideological mechanisms of social control. Says Oliver, "It was repressive in that it offered the possibility of forced removal from the community for anyone who refused to conform to the new order. But it was ideological also, in that it acted as a visible monument, replacing the public spectacle of the stocks, the pillory and the gallows, to the fate of those who would not or could not conform (1990, p. 48). The underpinning of this perspective was that as the medicalised control gains in proportion, it precipitates the notions of an able bodied individual. While this has the possibility of being true in India too, one noticeable feature was that though the medical definitions did gain prominence thereby controlling those who were not fit to pass the test, the kind of institutionalisation that the west saw was not there for the disabled people in India. Since the extended family support was and is still there, the removal of the disabled people from community life in India was not enacted. However, while on one hand this proved a boon, it was not without negative consequences. The families had to battle with the primarily negative imagery associated with disability.

The social model thus underpins the shifting of the onus from the individual to the society. As I have argued elsewhere people do not become disabled in a social vacuum. The subject thus, shifts from the disabled to the society, thus initiating a shift from 'them' to 'us'; approach in which the query is not as to what is wrong with them (the disabled) but to what is wrongs with 'us' i.e. the culture and the social system that has been organised (Ghai, 2000, pp.148-149). The social structuring of disability by socio-economic status, gender, location has been confirmed by a range of studies that show that disabled adults are likely to have low earnings or be unemployed. The clarity that in addition to the primary impairment, the disabled person faces a hostile environment designed for an 'able-bodied' society makes the questioning of a disabling environment a primary concern. Lack of access to communication, be it in the form of availability of Braille materials, augmentative measures or sign language training, heightens the oppression experienced by disabled persons.

The social model challenges the view that the human being is flexible and alterable, while society is fixed and unalterable. According to this approach, disability does not imply broken persons, but an inadequate society neatly tuned to the workings of normative structure serving political and economic ends. In this sense, the social model has been instrumental in emancipation of disabled lives. For instance, Liz Crow shares her relief, when what is perceived as her personal tragedy finds a rejection in the articulation of the social model. Says Crow, "This was the explanation I had sought for years. Suddenly what I had always known, deep down was confirmed. It wasn't my body that was responsible for all my difficulties; it was external factors, the barriers constructed by the society in which I live... Even more important, if all the problems had been created by society, then surely society could uncreate them. Re-evolutionary"! (Crow, 1996, p. 206).

An Alternative Suggestion

Mark Priestley (1998) suggests that both the individual and social models, can be further divided on the basis of their materialist or idealist emphasis. For instance, an individual model with a materialist orientation is concerned with the physical concomitants of impairment and the individual model with idealist orientation is concerned with the psychological connotations of impairment. Similarly, the materialist orientation of the social model emphasises that disability is the material product of socio-economic relations developing within a specific historical concept. The idealist orientation of the social model, on the other hand, reflects a concern with culture and representation. The four positions summarized by Priestley have been given in the following table (1998, p. 77).

	Materialist	**Idealist**
Individual	*Position 1* *Individual materialist models* Disability is the physical product of biology action upon the functioning of material individuals (bodies). The units of analysis are impaired bodies.	*Position 2* *Individualist idealist model* Disability is the product of voluntaristic individuals (disables and non-disables) engaged in the creation of identities and the negotiation of roles. The units of analysis are beliefs and identities.
Social	*Position 3* *Social creationist models* Disability is the material product of socio-economic relations developing within a specific historical concept. The units of analysis are disabling barriers and material relations of power.	*Position 4* *Social constructionist model* Disability is the idealist product of societal development within a specific cultural context. The units of analysis are cultural values and representations.

Social Construction of Disability

Various attempts have been made, within social model, to look at disability in terms of social construction. Though social construction has been explained in a number of ways, I refer to Peter Berger and Thomas Luckmann's work on *The Social Construction of reality*. They believe that humans produce their world, and themselves within their world through interaction with the environment. This process is essentially cognitive in nature, with language as a key adaptive role. As they say, "the developing human being not only interrelates with a particular natural environment, but with a specific cultural and social order, which is mediated to him by the significant others who have charge of him" (Berger and Luckmann, 1967, p. 48).

Susan Wendell too, in her book *The Rejected Body* for example, uses social construction and sees disability as socially constructed, "in ways ranging from social conditions that straightforwardly create illness, injuries and poor physical functioning to subtle cultural factors that determine standards of normality and exclude those who do not meet them from full participation in their societies" (Wendell, 1996, p. 36).

Similarly Robert Bogden and Steven Taylor illustrate the social construction of a typical severely disabled person in their study. They discuss the case of twenty year old Jean, who cannot walk or talk. As they elaborate further, "Her clinical records describe her as suffering from cerebral palsy and being profoundly retarded. Her thin, short— four feet long forty pound—body, atrophied legs and disproportionably large head makes her an unusual sight. She drools, rolls her head and makes seemingly incomprehensible high pitched sounds. But this is the way outsiders would describe her, the way we described her as sociologists encountering her for the first time. To Mike and Penny Brown, Jean's surrogate parents for the past six years, she is their loving and lovable daughter, fully part of the family and fully human" (Bogden and Taylor, 1989, p. 138). Thus, disability is a powerful social construct within most existing societies and because we are presented with conflicting images of it, disabled people have been placed into the role of the abnormal outsider whose lives and experiences are hidden from the 'normal' majority. These notions exist because of a tendency on the part of all human beings to view their own selves and each other from a particular perspective. The resulting constructions are inundated with meanings or value-laden ways of discerning at overt as well as unconscious levels of awareness. As these meanings are shared by a large number of people, they manage to create a strong consensus about the construction in question. This consensus is so deeply entrenched within the psyche that it comes to be understood as 'real' objective fact. Once it has been established as a fact, any attempt to say dislodge it as a mere perception is fraught with difficulties, as it is impossible to screen out what is deemed as purely objective and real. As Deborah Gallagher puts it, "things are what we make of them because we cannot disentangle things from meanings or distinguish facts from values" (Gallagher, 2001, p. 665). The critical issue therefore is that disability is used as an explanatory term depicting the appraisal or more accurately, a de-evaluative verdict brought to a given condition such as not being able to see, hear, read, think, memorise or act in accordance with culturally acceptable normal standards. Understanding disabilities as social constructions is not meant to underestimate the trauma experienced by disabled women. It must be acknowledged that difficulties are very real, indeed, but it does not imply that disability can exist without our beliefs, values and cultural understandings.

Within the Indian scenario, the meaning of disability needs to be negotiated as embedded in multiple cultural discourses, with subtle nuances. As I have written elsewhere (Ghai, 2002b, p. 6) in the popular media, disability is often portrayed as a 'lack' or 'deficit.. These assumptions are rooted in the dominant Hindu mythology where the two most popular epics *Mahabharata* and *Ramayana* carry the deprivation as well as negative images associated with disability. In the former; king Dhritrashtra is deprived of the throne because of his visual impairment. Another set of images associates disability with evil and as something to fear and as an expectation to be submissive. Within the stories of both the epics Mahabharata and Ramayana, the central turn comes with the interventions of an orthopaedically impaired man Shakuni and a dwarf woman, Manthra both being presented as evil.

The narratives generally depict disabled people as suffering the wrath of God, being punished for misdeeds that either they or their families have committed. Yet another strand conceives of disability as eternal childhood, where survival is contingent upon constant care and protection. Here, the emphasis is on images of dependency, thereby reinforcing the charity/pity model. This list, though not exhaustive, illustrates the underpinnings of a negative cultural identity. Historically, there are also narratives that indicate instances where disabled people were considered as children of God. This positioning provided spaces, in spheres of religion and knowledge, where the ability to transcend the body was a distinct possibility. Even though the implicit meaning of such possibilities may be disturbing within our present understanding of disability, it does indicate a dignified negotiation of difference. Thus, the renowned scholar Ashtvakra, who had eight deformities, and the great poet Surdas, who was visually impaired, are illustrations of strength and the ability to fight oppression. However, within these constructions, disability is something that can be overcome. All the same, the predominant cultural construction of disability is largely negative.

A Post-Modernist Approach to Disability

Another alternative approach for understanding disability has been offered by a group of feminists who show a definite inclination towards post modernist theories (See Mairian Corker, 1998; and Janet Price & Margrit Shildrick, 1996). The general consensus is that a conceptualisation of disability as a creation of society and culture is more aligned with the cultural and intellectual movements of post modernism, since these are the movements within which ideas of social constructionism have been formulated. Postmodernism challenges the idea that there can be one grand narrative of disability, which conveys a universal understanding of disability. Within the context of disability, Corker (1998, p. 232) delineates the viability of postmodernism in highlighting the relationship between individual and society, as opposed to a focus on the grand narrative of either. She suggests that postmodernism, or more specifically, poststructuralism, encourages us to work against the categories that the dominant culture uses to dichotomise the social realities. As I have written elsewhere (Ghai, 2002a, p. 89), "Postmodernism thus questions the oppositional character of discourse on social reality. The dominant ideologies in Indian culture have continued to operate paradoxically in characterising the binaries that define social realities. While in principle they might be postulated as complementary, their actual meaning/working is oppositional. Thus there is a strong cultural belief that while the female is opposed to the male, she is at the same time encompassed in the male. This is symbolised in representation of Lord Shiva as androgynous, Ardh Narishwar, where the left side is depicted as female and the right side as male. Similarly, *Purusha* (man)/*Prakriti* (nature), touchable/ untouchable, represent the same paradox". The binary of disability/ ability however, does not figure anywhere, as disability represents horror and tragedy. That the incomplete body is unwanted in Indian culture is evident from the reluctance of people to part with their body organs even after death. Postmodern theory, which measures its competence in terms of justice to heterogeneity, locality and complexity, can provide space that allows for multiple discourses. What is needed in India is an abandonment of the assumptions of essentialism, and concomitantly universalism, and the development of a vision of plurality that focuses on the wholeness of our own bodies. It is here that I feel, a poststructuralist theory can be of significance, to recognise that the disruption of a unified and individualistic subject is replaced with the indeterminate subject constituted and reconstituted in multiple ways. The freedom to understand the plurality and instability of experiential realities could offer creative possibilities for growth.

While I have introduced various theoretical positions to understand disability, a detailed analysis of their advantages and disadvantages is outside the purview of this book. My engagement with disability is as it impacts on gender. The following section will identify the debates that have relevance for a feminist understanding of disability.

The first issue is regarding the commonality versus specificity of disability. While it is true that the social model theories assert that disability has some real collective existence in the social world beyond the existence or experience of individual disabled people, the validity of this claim is premised upon the existence of some form of neutrally identifiable unity amongst disabled people. The argument while acknowledging the diversity of interest and identity between disabled people in terms of impairment, gender, 'race', age, class or sexuality, retains an essential level of commonality in the collective experience of discrimination and oppression.

While it is perfectly just to aim for a collective reality, it will be worthwhile to remember that theories are always constructed with specific perspectives conceived at particular times in history. Whether they reflect the current understanding of concepts in question is highly doubtful. Moreover, it is not mandatory that the theory will be comprehensive enough to incorporate issues with which all members of a specific constituency are concerned. As Corker says, "Social theories that are grounded in some notion of 'real' experience or which do their work by dichotomising experience and putting some notion of a real society outside of this experience, inevitably exclude other kinds of experience which are labelled as 'subjective' or 'ideal'. Perhaps, more importantly, notions of social agency, outside of those that are simply contrary to the hegemonic ideal, are sidelined. These realities will be of little use to those disabled people who feel their experience, beliefs and values have been rejected or to new social movements whose struggles hinge upon their articulation of a collective politic of resistance" (Corker, 1999, p. 628).

From my vantage point, as a disabled woman from the third world, I am weary of all encompassing generalisations about disability especially in a developing world. My contention is that the global community is an elusive one. As I contend elsewhere (Ghai, 2001a, p. 26), "Globalisation has constructed a world that offers open-ended possibilities and new life patterns, like access to information and technology. However, the paradox is that its emphasis on power and profit has systematically dislodged vulnerable groups from access to even basic resources such as food and livelihood. Consequently, this transformation of society has a very different meaning for people who have been oppressed because of their gender, class, race, religion, caste, displacement and disability status. As disability cuts across all categories, it has been suggested that it is a global issue, thus implying that its meaning and nuances are universal. However, there are serious problems with this understanding.

While I, who have access to the Internet and a hand driven car, can be considered a privileged disabled person, others in my country are fighting for their very basic survival needs. The idea that there are commonalities in all disabled lives, raises significant questions in a country like India. In the fight for rights, whose ideology and whose agenda it is, are more important questions. Just as who will determine the dominant cultural ethos and what kind of social systems will be sanctioned are critical issues. Answers to such questions in the third world are extremely complicated, considering the diversities of the various populations. An understanding of disability has therefore to be located within a specific context, in which a given disabled person is situated.

While the developed world has evolved to a point where it is demanding independent living for the disabled, the developing world is still enmeshed in struggles of basic survival issues for a large majority of the population. The term "access to resources" has a very different connotation in India as compared to either America the US or UK. Moreover, there is no discourse, which recognizes that classification of disability, which locates the problem and the solution within the individual, ignores structural oppression and discrimination such as poverty and physical and attitudinal barriers. However, within the developing countries the stress has been on the improvement of services. Such an approach neglects issues outside the world of service provision which make up the wider context of the lives of the disabled people. It won't be an exaggeration to say that poverty and the vicious cycle of poverty trap, exacerbates the experience of disability. The idea of the western theory being replicated in the Indian setting in a meaningful way therefore, has to be an extremely cautious assignment.

Another area of concern especially from a point of view of women has been the tendency to dichotomise impairment and disability. As early as 1976, Micheline Mason made the following observation regarding the disability movement in UK "I believe UPIAS[6] existed, and I was pleased to know that, but having been emotionally and intellectually battered to the floor by one of its leaders, it did not feel it was like anything to which I wanted to belong"(Mason, 1996, p. 52). Similarly Jenny Morris, a staunch supporter of the social model and the disability movement, says, "Like other political movements, the disability movement in Britain and throughout the world has tended to be dominated by men, both as theoreticians, and, as holders of important organisational posts" (Morris, 1991, p. 9).

Within India too, the domination of men and male concerns have dominated the disability movement. Any index, whether it is education, employment or marriage will clearly show that disabled men have featured more than disabled women. In the fights for visibility in society, inclusion in the census, discounted rates in the hotels, and other such contexts one can clearly see the middle class, male-centric concerns, that are guiding the development of the disability movement in India. The recognition that disability as an identity category has to be understood in relation to caste, class, religion, urban/rural divide and most importantly in relation to gender, are missing from research and analysis. This lacuna has been voiced by many thinkers, who were wary to accord disability a centrality, that would bypass other significant factors, such as class, caste, age and most importantly, type of disability. However, for many thinkers, specially the disabled feminists, the exclusion of the real experience of impairment is a very problematic one. In fact over the last decade disabled women have criticised the masculine bias of the disability movement and engendered theorising around disability issues. For example, Corker, while accepting the concept of disability as a form of social oppression problematises the foundations on which it has built the conceptual distinction between disability and impairment. These arguments resonate with disabled feminists such as French, Crow and Morris who recognise the centrality of impairment to a woman's existence. Sally French (1993) acknowledges

[6]UPIAS as explained earlier refers to the Union of Physically Impaired against the Segregation.

that the formation of a strong social movement requires people with widely differing impairments to present a coherent social definition of disability and expresses concern that personal experiences of impairment are not accommodated within this view. In a similar vein, I too stress that a disabled identity cannot overlook the material reality of the impaired body. "Should I blame this pain on society? Who can I demonstrate against? Not all bodily suffering is a socially curable phenomenon. Some physical pain is simply the consequence of having a body that's made of flesh. All living creatures know pain. Those of us living with disabilities may know more than most" (Ghai,1998, p. 36).

These concerns of pain, fatigue, depression and uncertainty do not find any resonance within the social model of disability. Yet these are the experiences, which set disabled people apart from other socially oppressed groups. In one important respect, there is nothing problematic about other marginalised categories as embodiment: sexuality, sex and skin colour are neutral facts. In a striking contrast, impairment actually signifies that the experiential realities the body can be intrinsically unliveable or difficult. Thus, conceptualising disability, as a social oppression might not be an appropriate theoretical framework for understanding the finer nuances of a life marked with disability.

My submission therefore is the material body, which is impaired, cannot be left out of the disability discourse. Within the framework put forward by disabled feminists from the west, this anomaly of linking impairment with the biological has been a cause for concern. The fear has been that recognition of the pain of impairment does not negate the fact that people with difference may be discriminated against collectively. Thus, both rationally and politically, there is a need to recognize that many disabled people are indeed challenged by acquired impairments. Impairments cannot be resolved only through legislations. Though essential, provision of services and accessible facilities alone cannot challenge the ablest hegemony, a change in the societal attitude towards a more positive construction of disability has to be coupled with the battle of rights. It is much simpler to talk about and devise strategies of discrimination in employment, and education than to talk about our experiences of exclusion from sexuality and reproduction. Some disabled people would even like to be cured of, or at least experience some respite from their condition. In fact a realisation of the embeddedness of disability in impairment, adds to an understanding of the complexities of a disabled person's identity.

I think it is imperative for contemporary disability theory to acknowledge that to negate ontological reality would imply that every issue connected with the disabled existence could be resolved with a change in the social conditions. Such an assertion will echo in the feminist debates that have emphasised the body as a major site for ideological contestations. Disabled bodies however have remained out of the feminist ambit. The disability theory by replicating this neglect has been as unjust as the mainstream feminist discourse. In the following chapters, I take a look at the experience of disability from the point of view of an 'impaired body' and understand the nuances of incorporating impairment within the theoretical endeavours of both the disability theory as well as the feminist discourse. While acknowledging that the issues might be equally critical for disabled men, my own vantage point are the disabled women. Before proceeding further, it is important to clarify the terminology utilised for this purpose.

A Note on Terminology

For feminism and disability theory, language is of critical importance to any discourse. It is indeed imperative for a feminist project to be extremely conscious of utilising politically correct language. Within the disability discourse, this concern assumes equal if not greater concern as the diagnostic categories commonly used within the disability discourse imply what Kenneth Gergen (1990) refers to as 'implicit hierarchies', which have the effect of reducing persons both in status and to the labels themselves. For Gergen, these labels operate to establish the essential nature of the person being described, and by which we understand the person in the world. The concern with the proliferating effects of the deficit vocabulary and maintenance of the very problems it attempts to describe, becomes fairly acute when one acknowledges the serious impact it has on the lives of disabled people. Thus, the activists and academics in disability studies have found it necessary to identify and intervene in the process through which both disabled persons and those who interact with them apply derogatory language. More so as this terminology then gets adopted by media representation thereby becoming part of the vernacular. A scrutiny of the terminology that is used in referring to those identified as physically or mentally different when compared with the so called normal, becomes imperative.

While different terminologies have been evolved, none of them have been accepted without considerable debate. Nuances between different terms such as the use of disabled people or people with disabilities have raised significant underlying assumptions. A number of objections have been raised with regard to terms such as invalid, confined to wheelchair, mentally retarded, blind and deaf and dumb. While the debates regarding terminology are important, for the present purpose, I have used the term-disabled individual thus placing the disability as the first categorical representation of that person/woman. I do this with the understanding that for a woman or a man, disability does become the central feature and the issue of personhood assumes secondary significance. I have thus used this phrase as an identity category for political reasons. My contention is that since society disables a person, a political process is required to undo the harm. Over the course of the last three decades or so, the term disabled people has been used when disability is referred to as a form of social oppression, experienced by people with perceived impairments and manifested in discriminatory practices (Priestley, 2001, xvii). This view is substantiated with the understanding derived from the Union of the Physically Impaired Against Segregation (UPIAS)/ Disability Alliance, 1976, p. 3). According to them, it is the society which disables by unnnecessarily isolating and excluding disabled persons from full participation in society. This is what makes the disabled people an oppressed group in society.

However, "person with a disability" has remained a preferred terminology within the formal structural systems that work with people with disabilities and also within most advocacy and political organizations, at least in India. The reasoning behind this is that the person with a disability is a person first, and the disability is incidental to that. It is a way of fighting against the stigma of disability and re-emphasizing the humanity, wholeness and normalcy of the person. The objective of the person first and disability second. Language is used thus to avoid the inherent objectification found within the term 'the disabled' and to escape what Dyer would call "the relentless parade of insults" (Dyer, 2001, p. 128) accomplished through the terms such as the cripple, the lame, the retarded, the blind, the spastic, or a collective, the handicapped. The origin of 'people first language' was rooted in the desire to create some distance between the person and the understanding that she/he is not completely determined by disability, which was/is mostly defined as a lack or deficit. However, the usage did not initiate change in the understanding of disability, which made its use somewhat problematic. A recent analysis by Tanya Titchkosky points out that in a subtle fashion "the person first approach" conceives of disability as a troublesome condition arbitrarily attached to some people, a condition (unlike gender, race or ethnicity) that is only significant as a remedial or managerial issue" (Titchkosky, 2001, p. 1). When conceived in this manner, the political advantage is lost, which for a feminist project seems too risky a proposition.

Within the Indian scenario, the terms disabled and handicapped have been used synonymously. Sometimes blind people have been referred to as Surdas, who, as mentioned earlier, was a great poet. Similarly *Mand Budhi* (developmental deficiencies) and *Viklang/apahij* (disabled/handicapped) have been used. Recently, Shridevi Rao (2001, p. 545), discussed the use of the word inconvenience by some of the Bengali mothers to describe a disabled child. The word inconvenience according to her defines the relationship of a non-disabled person toward the disabled person as being essentially characterised by support and acceptance. The word according to Rao also carries a moral imperative, which makes the non-disabled person's refusal to offer support to a person with inconvenience, a moral outrage. Though I agree with Rao to some extent, in my view the Indian society's transition from an autonomous one to a globalised economy has eroded many such values.

A recent analysis by Viewers Forum on Disability (2001) indicates that media continues to use the terms *Langra/langri/* (cripple) *aandha/aandhi* (blind) *behra* (deaf) and *pagal* (mentally insane) for the cognitive impairment. Perhaps it is Rao's location as a visitor from America, which is responsible for her too optimistic views regarding social attitudes towards disability in India. The reality is that disability is still used more as a metaphor, thus stripping away the questioning of the ethical prepositions, involved in the language debate. I am reminded of a fellow disabled Robert DeFelice indicating his preference for the historical word crippled. DeFelice says, "Crippled was good. Cripples have class, it sounds like Victorian back bedrooms. I like that. It's got mystery" (DeFelice as cited in Mitchell and Synder 1996). My intention definitely is not to advocate the use of the word cripple, but just to convey that any terminology, which makes the disabled reject the language of deviance for a language of pride, self worth and power, is to be welcomed.

2

Disabled Women: Issues, Concerns and Voices from Within

Gender is implicated in a disastrous and oppressive fiction, the fiction of "woman" which runs roughshod over multiple differences among and within woman who are ill-served by a conception of gender as basic.

Christine Di Stefano (1990, p. 65)

The last decade has been a testimony to the relentless efforts of disabled people in India. Disability legislation, inclusion in census and representations in media are some of the features of this struggle. Even though the legislative framework is not as strong as the disabled would have liked it to be, one has to acknowledge that it is only when the laws get stipulated, that space for participation in wider society, formerly denied to the disabled, can be provided. Though the pace is slow and efforts fragmented, nevertheless some visibility has been attained for the lives marked as disabled in a society that still largely ignores their existence. However, as I stated in the introduction, I re-stress the fact that even these miniscule efforts are guilty of ignoring the concerns of disabled women. Their voices have been subsumed by the male leaders, who have largely reflected their masculine bias by completely overlooking concerns such as sexuality, family and motherhood. My intention is to highlight the fact that notwithstanding the delay in the introduction and consequent implication of the disability legislation, one fact that often goes unnoticed is that out of the twenty-eight chapters of the disability legislation, not a single chapter concerns itself with the issues that specifically confront disabled women.

In a society where the gender ratio is steadily declining because of continuing female infanticide, life as a disabled woman cannot be an easy proposition. As I undertake this exercise of charting out the concerns of the disabled women, I wish to reiterate that while there is a certain commonality of experiences that disabled women all over the world might share, the cultural nuances cannot be ignored. Within the western scenario, though disabled women may not have emerged significantly in the feminist project, they have struggled to have their voices heard. However, in India, apart from a few attempts [Ghai, 2002c; Anuradha Mohit (Personal Communications); Preeti Mehra, 2000] voices and concerns have largely remained unexpressed, scattered, and consequently fragmented. While the language of rights that a male-centric approach tends to use is an important tool for political action, it can pose difficulties for women who feel that the personal experience of impairment is as crucial as the experience of social oppression. I hope that readers will realise that the reason for this is not a lack of resistance but the innumerable accessibility problems faced by disabled women placed in a disabling environment. These debar their entry into the able–mainstream world defined by patriarchal norms that under different circumstances could have become the platform for sharing their experiences from within the disembodied space marked as 'different'. It is within this conservative and gendered cultural scenario, that I locate disabled women in India. What follows in the chapter is based on a few narratives collected as part of an ongoing post-doctoral project on the lives of disabled women that I have been associated with for some time.

Charting the Concerns of Disabled Women in India

Difficult Childhood

Children within the Indian scenario as in many other parts of the world are conceived of as lineage and economic capital. The idea of lineage capital goes back to traditional expectations, which attaches the gender of the new born to familial and socio-cultural prospects. Each member of the family is thus under core obligations, that demand that he/she contributes to both the economic as well as the socio-cultural development of family and by extension the society in which she/he is embedded. In this kind of cultural setting the birth of a baby receives disproportionate welcome depending on the sex of the child. In India, the birth of a girl child is perceived as a liability. The desire for a son remains unparalleled culturally. Says Sudha Bhogle (1999, p. 295), "Being a mother of a legitimate offspring especially a son was considered to be the highest status woman could aspire for, and women are honoured for this family role". According to Rachana Johri (1998) the yearning for sons has to be understood in the cultural context of the ritualistic value of sons as well as the social and economic cost of bringing up the daughters.

Indian readers of course would understand this desire only too well. As Veena Das has said, "It is true that sons are seen as future heirs, and parents look upon them for support in their old age. In contrast, girls are seen as belonging to a different family altogether and their socialization stresses their future role as wives. However, daughters never cease to be the repositories of their family honour and though parents cannot depend on them for a fulfilment of material needs, they do look upon them as symbols of the honour of their families. The prestige of a family is in the hands of its daughters is a common refrain which a girl may expect to hear many times a day from her parents" (Das, 1979, p. 90). The construction of disabled children as lacking and deficient, is an idea, that precludes that they have no economic or social value attached to them (Ghai, 2001a, p. 27). In such a context, the birth of a disabled girl child is devastating and full of excruciating pain. Since disabled girls are seen as dependent and passive, the double burden of looking after them definitely is an avoidable proposal, as it symbolises a fate worse than death.

"Ek to ladki oopar se apahij, is se to accha mar jaati" (a disabled girl is better dead than alive) marks the reality of a woman with disability in India. As a six-year-old girl affected with polio says, "My mother says, *ek to ladki ka janam, oopar se yeh musibat. Patta nahin yeh mere kis janam ki sazza hai* (My mother laments that a disabled daughter is a punishment, and she cannot figure out what past sins are responsible for my disabled existence).

Leading a stigmatised life, a disabled woman in India belongs to a marginalised and invisible category. Whether disability is congenital or acquired, the oppression starts very early in life. With no opportunities for improving the quality of life, the disabled girl-child has no option but to live a life of subordination. Meena[1], a 10 year old girl, shares her experience of disability. An excerpt from my interview with Meena underpins the harsh reality of being labelled as a disabled girl child in India.

> Meena a ten-year-old girl got an attack of polio at a young age. Her parents, a middleclass couple worked extremely hard to give Meena a decent education. In their belief that a public school would be ideal, they sent her to a very well known school in the neighbourhood. What they did not realise is, that, even private schooling does not guarantee sensitivity towards their child's disability. Meena recalls her time in school, as follows: "I always wondered why god made me different. I hated going to school. Everyone use to call me *langri* (cripple). Even though that was bad enough, worse was the humiliation that the teacher would inflict on me, when I expressed my need to go to the toilet. Despite the fact that my class teacher knew that a fair distance had to be covered to reach the toilet, she would not grant me the permission. I had to literally plead, but she would remain unmoved. The other classmates were not made to go through the same treatment. The delay in the permission to get out would make me lose control either in the classroom or in the corridor. It was then that my nightmare would start in earnest. The teacher would give me a tight slap and tell all the students in the class about my loss of control. As if this was not enough she would then make them chant, "Shame shame, poppy shame. All the children know your name". Hearing them say this I would often wish that I were dead. To this day the aftermath of the nightmare remains, voices reverberate and I often feel the physical pain of the slapping by the teacher. I am not sure why she behaved like this. I guess it has to do with people's attitudes towards disability! Anyway, now I am determined to fight this battle, as I don't think that it is my fault that I have polio.

Needless to add, Meena carries scars that have not healed. Her narrative clearly indicates how the voice is silenced by the internalisation of the dominant and powerful social voice which conveys to her that she has absolutely no right to demand even what is rightfully her own. Her situation is a sad reflection of the stigma attached to disabled lives in Indian schools that provide education to a barely 2% to 7% of 30 million children in the age range of 5 to 14. As I have written

[1] The names have been changed to keep the original identities confidential.

elsewhere (Ghai, 2001a, p. 30), without education and employment, disability is a burden women can do without. In such a context it is not difficult to understand a father's lament in a remote village of Bihar. Says Guru, "Wasn't it enough that we are poor. Why did *kismet* (fate) have to add to our burden further by giving us a *pagal* (term used for mentally disable) daughter. She has made both my life and death difficult" (Personal Communication). It is not difficult to sense the insecurity, uncertainty and anxiety that his disabled daughter produces in him. And, as it often happens, wittingly or unwittingly, these feelings get communicated to the child, reducing her self-worth forever. What is significant is that the kind or severity of disability does not seem to make a difference, as the physically disabled girls are considered a curse. As is clear from Meena's interview, even when educational opportunities come they are not without the stigma attached to disability. Embedded in a matrix of poverty and disability the disabled girls rarely develop job related skills.

The educational policy of the Indian government recommends special education for the disabled. Thus without questioning the resource crunch, and a context where half of the so-called normal population of children in the country remain out of school, (two thirds of these are girls), special education can never be a viable option. (See Anil Sadgopal, 2000, p. 251; Ghai, 2001a, p. 32). Integration is an illusory concept in a country where schools continue to marginalise children for being different. Lack of education adds to the jeopardy that these girls are already in, because of the devaluation inherent in disability, that serves as one of the most powerful reasons used to legitimise the silencing of disabled girls/women, which is rarely challenged. Even if the opportunities are there, sometimes the limitations are so grave, that a disabled girl cannot help but think that it would have been better had she not been born. As Reema, a 14 year old shares her agony:

> I had cerebral palsy at birth. I am dependent on my parents and elder sister for everything. I cannot dress, eat or go to the toilet without help. The spastic society allowed me to study till class sixth. After that I am at home with my parents. Right now since they are there, I am O.K. However, after they die, I do not know what will happen to me. All the time, I just watch television. My

house is on the second floor, so even if my parents don't say no to going out, I myself say no. It is such an effort for them to take me out. I also have affected my sister's life, as she has to help in the housework. Few days back, I overheard my parents discussing the possibility of getting my uterus removed, so that I will not have periods. I cried a lot, but I know I am helpless.

While I have shared some narratives, concern with the ramifications of disability on education, work, school, social and emotional functioning seems to be a universal feature of growing up with disability. Being defined unidimensionally and primarily by disability, to which gender is added, creates an internal struggle for those who engage in the process of understanding both their limitations and grope in the dark to locate their strengths. As an 8 year old asks, "Didi, (elder sister) why did god do this to me/ I know that my parents love my brother more because he is not a burden for them. But was it my fault that I became disabled. Will I ever be loved as other children are loved and cared for"? (Personal Communication). Despite hardships, the family is the agency that provides emotional strength—although emotional bonding may be unexpressed, subterranean, unrealised or unarticulated. The specific emotional expression may change. What is important is that, despite the odds, there is relatedness within the family that sustains the subsistence of a disabled child, whether it is a boy or a girl. Though there may be a temporary loss of agency, the resilience of close family ties makes it possible to generate the necessary resistance to fight ongoing oppression.

Nonavailability of Traditional Roles

While some of the issues such as education, and the feeling of being a burden might be common to many young girls in India, once the girls reach puberty, a major preoccupation for parents in general is to find a suitable marriage partner for the girl, as culturally, the mark of womanhood is the ability to get married and reproduce. As Seemanthini Niranjana says in her book, *Gender and Space*, "The pressing obligation on the part of the parents, to marry off a girl underlines the high cultural value attached to wifehood... Often, a woman's space is inseparable from her understanding and acceptance of what is culturally defined as her dharma (duty) including her duties as a daughter, wife and mother" (Niranjana, 2001, p. 64). Though disability renders this task very difficult, most of the parents do attempt to search for a partner who would marry their daughter. However, marriage is not possible without giving a dowry. This practice constructs even the 'normal' daughter as a burden, conceiving her as *parai* (belonging to another/Another's). As Johri elaborates in her reading of *Manusmriti*, "one of the dharmic duties of the father is Kanyadan, (Johri, 1998, p. 78) the unreciprocated gifting of the virgin, to the husband and the family. Ideally the gift is such that nothing is taken in return. Kanyadan takes place in a complex set of rituals that involve varied symbolisms". The daughter is said to become her husband's *ardhangni* (other half). Giving dowry becomes a part of this ritual. And as the bride becomes the other, she now becomes a suitable object for *daan* (donation). The implicit understanding in this practice is that whatever you are gifting will be perfect. In case it happens to be a disabled girl, you have to compensate accordingly.

Ironical as it is, the neglect of the disabled woman from the psyche of even liberal feminists who consciously and zealously fight the patriarchal oppressions is such that while the *Manusmriti* has been read and re-read on a number of occasions, it is difficult to find any published work that has looked at it from the point of view of the disabled girl/woman. While many authors have interpreted traditional texts such as *Manusmriti*, for the present purpose I follow the interpretation by Wendy Doniger and Brian, K Smith (1991). *Law 72* in the text, states, "Even if a man has accepted a girl in accordance with the rules, he may reject her if she is despised, ill, or corrupted, or if she was given with something concealed". This is followed by *Law 73* which says, "If anyone gives away a daughter with a flaw and does not mention it, that gift from the evil hearted daughter-giver may be annulled" (Doniger and Smith, 1991, pp. 205–206).

Consequently, a culture in which arranged marriages are the rule inherently puts disabled woman in a difficult position. While there is a possibility of resistance, (however difficult) to this cultural arrangement for 'normal' women, for disabled girls, it is an uphill task. Some disabled girls in the rich or middle class contexts might be able to negotiate the difficulties in arranged marriages, albeit with a great deal of compromising. Disabled sons retain the possibility of marriage, as they are not gifts but the receivers of gifts. Disabled as well as non-disabled men seek 'normal' women as wives, and therefore participate in the devaluing. This is also reflective of the gendered character of the traditional set up which devalues the 'female' persona.

Even for those disabled women who have been fortunate enough to get proper education and are in some sense settled professionally, the humiliation of being disabled in the arranged marriage scenario is insurmountable. Urvashi, a well-placed bank employee shared her experiences at the time when her parents were desperately trying to get her married.

> Urvashi, a polio affected girl, recalls the horrors of the trauma she went through, when her parents advertised in matrimonial columns of a national daily. Within the dominant north Indian family where Urvashi is placed, advertising in the news papers is rated as negative. It reflects the girl' inability to find a husband. All the same, after making sure that the disability of the girl would be acceptable, the next issue concerned her earning ability. It is as if the penalty for the fate of disability is to be compensated with money. Though a lot has been written about the inherent objectification associated with the arranged marriage scenario, the repercussions for disabled girls, once again are often ignored. For Urvashi the entire experience was full of pain and humiliation. Notwithstanding the boy's mobility impairment, Urvashi had to be paraded before his entire family and relatives. She recalls vividly the scene when the boy's mother asked her to walk around from one room to another, evaluating whether she had enough mobility to serve the family members in the house. As if this were not enough, she wanted to inspect Urvashi's leg by asking her to lift her *salwar* (Indian Pants) with the objective of assessing the damage. Urvashi's beautiful face did not compensate for her very visible disability. If it did, it was when her parents also entertained a proposal from a mother whose son was a drug addict, in addition to being orthopaedically impaired. These experiences of recurrent humiliation were enough to discourage Urvashi from ever getting married. Another instance that still haunts her is when a boy with whom she grew up wanted to propose to her. His family, which treated her affectionately till then, suddenly withdrew. Urvashi, who seemed acceptable as a friend, was not right as a daughter-in-law. The label of disability did not leave any room for a 'normal' relationship. Their consequent hostility left scars on Urvashi's inner psyche. She not only lost intimate neighbours, but also a trusted friend. Says Urvashi, "I have accepted my fate. But how I wish that I could have known the joy of carrying a child".

My contention is that Urvashi's narrative speaks volumes for those countless narratives of many more such women who have remained unheard. The predominant Hindu tradition and culture defines women within a matrix or roles that are interpersonal in nature (Rao, 1969). Their identity is solely determined by their relationships to the significant others, be it, the father, husband or son. Disabled girls however find it exceedingly difficult to occupy even these privileged spaces. The noted sociologist M.N. Srinivas (1978) has commented that the Indian culture has venerated women in terms of the roles they play, but her individuality as a 'woman' in her own right is hardly ever valorised. In such circumstances, the socialisation process, which is derived from the practices of gender inequality, is translated into the everyday lives of women. In addition to these cultural constructions, disability has an adverse impact especially on the poorer and the low caste sections, who get marginalised when multiple labels become interactive. Thus a poor dalit girl who is disabled slips lower and lower in the hierarchy of roles. Anita's voice captures the pain of being poor and disabled.

> As Anita, a girl from a low socio-economic class, who has not been educated, says, my fate was sealed the day I was born with a very mild attack of cerebral palsy. How can my parents accumulate enough money to marry me off? Even those men, who have been married earlier, demand money for me. My father beats me up, as there is no respite for him. I cannot even help him in the family, as I am unable to get a job. I have hardly ever stepped out of the house, since, I don't even have the money to get myself a pair of crutches, and I am bound to this one room house. Even my own brother calls me *apahij* (disabled). Only if God would be kind enough to take me away from this world.

Anita's pain is a testimony to unprecedented pressures that disability places on girls. The problems get accentuated when disabled men too want non-disabled wives. The desire could perhaps be understood in terms of the metaphor of 'seed' and 'earth' discussed by Leela Dube (1986). In terms of the metaphor, seed and earth represent the respective contribution of the male and female in biological reproduction. The implications of these metaphors for the positioning of women within a patriarchal system in pre-dominant agrarian economies illustrate how these symbols reinforce essentially unequal relationships. Dube further highlights the underplaying attributed to women's contribution to biological reproduction, and thereby legitimising man's rights over women's sexuality and reproductive capacity as well as property and productive resources. That the symbolic and material are inextricably linked, notwithstanding the man's disability is clearly evident from Sanwari's narrative. It depicts the pain and anguish of being not considered as 'right' even by the fellow disabled.

> Sanwari, a visually impaired woman, works in a reputed school. She has a reasonably good education, because of the concerted efforts of her mother. While her childhood and young adulthood was marked with the stigma of being blind, her pain became acute when she reached marriageable age. Says Sanwari, "Visually impaired men prefer sighted wives. It is not difficult for them to achieve this goal, as there are many poor families who are willing to marry their daughters to visually impaired man, especially if they have a sound job or financial backing. But it is very rare for a sighted man to marry a blind woman: there is generally a very special commitment or reason for it. However, I do not perceive myself as a person who is blind. And if I go around pitying myself, I would lose my self-respect. I don't want to do that. I think of myself as capable as the so called 'sighted'. In fact as I live my life on a day to day basis, I don't remember that I am blind, though it is very clear to me that it is obvious to the world.

Recently, Veena Das & Renu Addlakha (2001) presented the case of a woman called Mandira, who was considered impaired on account of a birthmark covering half her face, but considered normal in all other aspects. Das goes on to share Mandira's narrative and comments that, "The aspect of impairment that caused her parents the most anxiety was its impact on marriage prospects. Indeed, within the wider kinship network, Mandira's birthmark was seen as a major misfortune for her parents, since most of their relatives considered it extremely unlikely that a suitable husband could be found for her. It is thus not difficult to imagine the state of those disabled girls, who have disabilities that are much more serious than a birthmark" (Das and Addlakha, 2001, p. 515).

Another issue that was highlighted in the narratives I gathered was that the availability of the traditional roles such as marriage, was dependent on class. Belonging to the rich, middle-class determines the experiential reality of disability. If the family can afford it, the daughter will be provided with education. Otherwise the attempt is to search for institutionalisation, so that not many people know of her existence. Later if she does manage to become employed, poor families are not keen on the disabled girl's marriage as that also implies losing the income. Once again, this is the reality of many girls who belong to poor households. The family is at least under societal pressure to get the girls married. But in case of the disabled girls, the societal pressure is not there, which helps the parents to become as oppressive as the able society. In such instances, either the disabled girl chooses to stay and cater to the family wishes, or, she is left to her own devices to find a marriage partner. That itself can be a difficult proposition.

> Beena, a woman who had polio at an early age was given education in a government school. Being a bright student, she managed to get a scholarship to go through college. Once she got a stable job, she expressed a desire to get married. However, her parents were not very happy about her decision. Says Beena, "I was reminded about my disability. They asked me to recall that they brought me up with great difficulties. Now I was made to feel like a thankless daughter, who was refusing to take care of them. My father said that it was my moral duty to take care of them in their old age. When I would remind them of my sister, they would point out to my disability, and say that why were you not born 'normal' like her? My brother on the other hand was allowed to get married and live separately with his wife. I was reminded about my obligations each day and I was expected to be grateful because they did not send me away to an institution. I am now stuck with this situation. I joined 'Family of the Disabled,[2] to enable me meet people who are like me. However, my parents get angry when I step out to attend their meetings. I feel so lonely but I guess I just need to be stronger than what I am.

The richer or the middle class disabled might be able to negotiate such a dilemma, though not without compromise. Social class presents a different picture as education is prioritised as a prime goal by parents for both sons and daughters and is clearly perceived as a pathway to success (See Kakar and Chowdhry, 1970; Sharma, 1996).

[2]Family of the Disabled is an N.G.O run by Rajinder Johar, a quadraplegic.

Disha, a woman with cerebral palsy recalls with an indifferent stance, "I am forty years old. To date, my father has never exchanged a word with me. I have caused a loss of his honour. All he does is that he provides financially for me". Even though Disha attempts to downplay the impact, her sense of rejection and the pain that she experiences is not very difficult to comprehend. She believes that for her father she is a non-existent entity. The saving grace of her life have been her grandparents who have looked upon her as God's gift and have bestowed all the love and affection on her. The matters became worse, when Disha's boyfriend another disabled person, told her clearly that as far as marriage is concerned, he would only marry a non–disabled girl.

However, even financial support does not make it easy for the disabled women. Even when the parents do manage to get the girl married after giving a lot of dowry, the stigma of disability does not get washed away so easily. The notion of giving also implies that it is easier to get matches for the sons, as the dowry does not have to be given. In a scenario like this, the disabled males become as oppressive as the normal society, as most of them do not consider disabled women as potential life partners.

As Anjali who had been married to another impaired person with a lot of dowry says, "Every moment of my marriage, I had to listen to the fact that I was useless. On reminding my husband that he too is impaired, I was chucked out of the house. I tried turning to my parents for help. However, they told me to keep quiet. Finally I went to the police. The officer took one look at me and said, *Arre bhai, tumhe to uska shukargujar hona chaiye langri aurat ho kar bhi shor machati ho* ("Be grateful for the fact that he married you what can the poor guy do with a lame girl..".). Later on the case went to the court, which could not manage to get even my personal things back. I now live in a hostel with a job which barely looks after my needs. All the same Anjali continues to wear a Mangalsutra (symbol of a married woman) around her neck and keeps a fast for the long life of her husband.

Given the significance of being married, Anjali's reactions though ironical are understandable. For those who do manage to get this highly valorised role of being married, further dilemmas confront them with regard to the possibilities of motherhood. Within the dominant Indian ethos, says Sudhir Kakar, "Whether her family is poor or wealthy, whatever her caste, class or *religion*, whether she is a fresh young bride or exhausted by many pregnancies and infancies already, an Indian woman knows that motherhood confers upon her a purpose and identity that nothing else in her culture can. Each infant borne and nurtured by her safely into childhood, especially if the child is a son, is both a certification and a redemption" (Kakar, 1978, p. 56). However, it is also a culture which privileges only legitimate motherhood. Any desire to have a child out of wedlock is deemed to evoke further stigmatisation. However, disabled women are denied the possibility of even this very prestigious role, as marriage and motherhood are both difficult aspirations.

> Shalini's parents were elated when a sighted man offered to marry her. She was told to thank God, as it was only due to his grace that someone was motivated to marry her. Her parents visited holy shrines to express their gratitude. It was only then, that Shalini realised the extent of their apprehensions regarding her disabled existence. The family which till then appeared to be an ideal family suddenly lost its charm as Shalini understood that all along she had been a burden for them. Notwithstanding her well paid job, her worth was in terms of whether she could get married. Consequently her husband was constructed as benevolent and she the recipient of his selfless gesture. Says Shalini, "I was told over and over again that motherhood was not for me. What if the child also turns out to be blind like you. Haven't I had enough to be saddled with a disabled wife? Don't make it unbearable by imposing a disabled child on me". Despite the fact that Shalini is a well-established professional, she finds herself unable to fight this battle. Says Shalini, "My husband becomes hostile the moment I express my desire to become pregnant. Now I have accepted fate, but sometimes, I want to break this trap. I have even got all the tests done to assure him that my disability is not genetic, still he remains adamant".

While it is perfectly justified for the feminists to engage with the issues of natural and constructed motherhood, the pain and agony of women like Shalini goes unheard. The rationality of genetics in such a scenario is hardly ever questioned. Even the non-disabled women are blamed for giving birth to girls, while it is the male genes that determine sex. The position of disabled women is not hard to imagine. A fallout of this scenario is that the use of genetic technology in its different forms in cases of disability remains out of the ambit of public discourse. Though defined as 'preventive' for many disabled people, the measures are an expression of the essence of the personal tragedy model, positing a "better dead than disabled" approach.

In India, the technological advances such as genital screening have created a eugenic movement that might be unheard of in the west. The desire for a son has translated into abortions of the female foetus. While the west has vehemently protested against the killing of the disabled infants in India, the preference for sons has resulted in a lowest ever sex ratio (census 2001). Says Krishanji, "Unless sex determination and female infanticide are halted, there is a distinct possibility for a further loss of girls" (Krishanji, 2000, p. 1161). This becomes clearly evident in the Indian women's movement campaign against amniocentesis, as a sex determination test leading to female foeticide. While there have been plenty of debates, within feminism, that argue about the ethical contradictions involved in killing female foetuses, as well as the right to abort, the use of the test as a genetic screening test for diagnosing disabled children has not been addressed (Menon, 1996). Coupled with the predominant negative presumptions held about impairment and disability, it is not in the least surprising that the abortion of impaired foetuses does not even find a mention in these debates.

While I am deeply concerned with the killing of disabled infants, I am certainly not questioning the choice of abortion being available to women in general. However, I do wish to point out the nuances of these choices in a society where, disability is only conceived of as a medical and not a social problem. The most serious form of these developments are being manifested in projects such as the 'human genome' which are intended to map the entire genetic code to get rid of all those conditions that are conceived of, as disabling, incurable and genetically transmitted. It is true that gender is not a genetic defect, and sex selection violates the principle of equality between females and males, and the attitude of unconditional acceptance of a new child by parents, (so psychologically crucial to parenting). However, in a country where sex selection is an acceptable precedent for "genetic tinkering" at parental/cultural whim, for characteristics that are unrelated to any disease, how an actual genetic defect, would stand the test remains debatable (Ghai, 2001b, p. 25). The question thus is, who decides what is a defect and what is not. Obviously, the need is for the feminist discourse to understand that rules for discrimination have to be better drawn. Simply put, gender based discrimination in one class and discrimination related to all other potentially perceived factors in another category will not suffice. The dangers faced by the disabled foetuses in such a division would not ask for too much imagination

Notwithstanding the genetic tinkering, the respite for disabled women does not come even when decisions to adopt are considered, as such options are not available to them. A well placed professional woman Sheila shares her experience at thus:

> When my family failed yet again in arranging a match for me, I gave up on the idea of getting married. However, the desire to bring forth a child was very strong in me. As a result, I went to an adoption agency. They took one look at my disability and informed me in certain terms that, I was ineligible for adopting a child. "They would rather have children living without mothers. A disabled mother was not their idea of providing parental love to the orphaned children!"

These issues of marriage and motherhood are further accentuated by the disengagement from the disability discourse of those few successful disabled women who manage to find careers or happy marriages. Their disassociation implies a negation of disability, as very few contest the dominant constructions or become advocates of their life situation. That the situation is similar in the west is stressed by Meekosha (1998, p. 166) who indicates that women with disabilities are reluctant to share their personal stories, in the fear that they might be seen as spectacles. The late Irving Zola called this denial the 'structured silence of personal bodily experiences' (Zola, 1998, p. 166). This illustrates the marginality of a disabled identity. The sense of internalised oppression that it creates is too difficult to handle. Renuka who is a well placed doctor abhors the idea of ever being called disabled. According to her, "Everyone has problems, so why should I highlight my disability. I have always tried to overcome the obstacles. I do not wish to become a story for the press" (Personal Communication). Similarly many disabled women who have attained a certain status in life refuse to even admit that they are disabled. While this might be an excellent illustration of the 'overcoming', it certainly does not help in raising the issue in the wider society.

In a context, where marriage and motherhood are seen as compulsory for women, denial of the traditional roles can only be termed oppressive. What might be conceived by the feminists as the traditional roles are denied to disabled women, creating, what Fine and Asch (1988, p. 14) call 'rolelessness'—a social obscurity and annulment of femininity that can prompt disabled women to claim the female identity valorised by the given cultural prescriptions. Disabled men on the other hand, escape hopelessness by 'redefining their adeptness at the male role', where perfecting the female sex role only reinforces the stereotypical, passive disability role'.

> As Varsha who has muscular dystrophy says, "My parents discuss me as if I am not there. All I have for company is the television, but there too, I can only watch those programmes, which my older sister feels like watching. Since I am disabled, my parents and siblings treat me like a burden to be borne with. Whether it is food or studies, I am always the last on the list of their priorities. Since I can never be the daughter they want and I cannot get married, I do not have any role in life". Totally dependent on her servant, Varsha shares her alienation and dejection with her fellow disabled friends and expresses a keen desire to die early.

Issues of (A)Sexuality

In my interviews with disabled women, the most difficult discussions were around sexuality. Mostly the issue of sexuality did not appear on their horizon as a significant issue as being disabled did. Like most Indian women, sexuality was defined within the parameters of marriage. Most of the disabled women found themselves without words to express their sexuality. In a culture where any deviation from a norm is seen as a marked deviation, the impaired body becomes a symbol of imperfection. The myth of the beautiful body defines the impaired female body as unfeminine and unacceptable. The roots of such thinking are found in Indian mythological instances, where Lakshmana, brother of lord Rama, cuts off the nose of 'Shurpanakha' sister of King Ravana, who is interested in him. That Lakshmana can only respond to what he defines as non-acceptable behaviour by disabling the ugly female monster indicates how disability and desexing are equated in the Indian psyche. The ramifications of such historical rendering are to be found in the North Indian Punjabi culture, where, for instance, girls though allowed to interact with their male cousins, are not allowed to sleep in the same room. Disabled girls, on the other hand, are under no such prohibitions, as they are considered sexually safe, or asexual (Ghai, 2002c). The assumption is that they will not conceive of the interaction as a 'come on signal' nor invite a sexual encounter. It is almost as if a disabled girl is perceieved not like other girls but is 'above all that', which has the effect of freeing the other to imitate any action, which in more cases than most turns out to be exploitative. As the personal narrative of Simi reveals:

> When I was young, I would be thrilled at being allowed to sleep in the same room as Vipin, who was my first cousin. However, as I grew up, I realised that this benevolent gesture of my family was to be understood as a complete de-sexualization of my body. Later that same cousin proposed me and said that he was willing to satisfy my sexual desires, if I promised to keep quiet and not publicise the illicit liaison.

This reflects what Hahn (1997, p. 25) calls 'asexual objectification'. It also highlights the disregard of the dangers of sexual violation to which disabled girls are exposed. Although never reaching the headlines, there are enough instances, where their own fathers and uncles have sexually abused disabled girls. As one of my informants, whose sister has cerebral palsy revealed:

> My sister always had problems in communicating because of speech problems. However after her school gave argumentative aids to her, she shared with me an experience, which was absolutely horrifying. At first, I did not believe her, yet her tears finally convinced me. My Dad's younger brother took advantage of the fact that both my mother and I had to leave town for work and college. As there was no school, which would accept her after the age of 13, we had to leave her at home. He stayed with us for a month, and my sister became a wreck during that time. However, as she could not communicate, we attributed her agitation to her disability. It was only later that we came to know how he raped her

everyday for a month or so. The maid who was to take care of her also cooperated with him for money. Even after this episode, my father refused to break his relationship with his brother. After being threatened that we all would commit suicide, he stopped visiting our house.

While this is one side of the story, the assumption that sexuality and disability are mutually exclusive also denies that people with deviant bodies experience sexual desires and need sexual fulfilment. I personally found my growing years as marked by this belief As I have shared elsewhere, (Ghai, 1998). "There were times when guys on the street would whistle and make some remarks, which in those days was thought of as harassment (no one could have anticipated the real meaning of the term). Where my feminist friends would protest, I could never share with them that I wanted to soak in every lustful look. In fact, along with my only other disabled friend, I would literally savour every obscene word".

Castelnuovo & Guthrie describe how disabled bodies are constructed as asexual. They submit, "Although the notion of fluid sexuality, which includes the possibility of asexuality, is likely to be intriguing to a postmodernist feminist bent on deconstructing sexual identity, the idea of not being sexually attractive to anyone or having no sexual options sexually attractive whatsoever is likely to be disconcerting" (Castelnuovo and Guthrie, 1998, p.131).

Mothering a Disabled Daughter

The stigma attached to disabled girls and women has not left their mothers unblemished. They too have not escaped the torture which accrues to them for having given birth to disabled daughters. Once again the feminist discourse in India has paid scant attention to the issue of women who are the mothers of disabled children, specially girls. When women cannot validate their social status only as mothers who bore healthy children for their husband's family, those who give birth to disabled children are condemned to live in shame. There have been enough instances where, women have been divorced, left and tortured because they have given birth to a disabled child. Given the preference for sons even here, the 'mother blaming' is more severe in instances of a girl child.

The narratives of mothers who have spastic and developmentally disabled daughters, are reflective of pain and anguish, that they experience with a disabled daughter. (Arora and Ghai 1997; Mangla and Ghai 2000). While their experiences are complicated, what emerges clearly is their frustration, with lack of awareness and understanding in society. Most of them felt that they were constructed as pitiable and peculiar. Some, commented on how their efforts to lead a normal life were hampered by the attitudes of their relations. 'Karma Theory' has been a significant part of their narratives. The 'disabled child' is seen as a retribution for the 'past karmas' (actions). There have been times when the mothers have been blatantly told that they are cursed. Mrs Duggal, the parent of a disabled girl agonises:

> A very close relative of mine told me that my daughter's illness was a result of the curse that she had given me, when I annoyed her over something. I felt distraught. Even if I cause some harm to someone, I will not go and say this to her. Others said that it was a result of my bad actions (*bure karma*). Educated people would laughingly tell me that our children were saying that she looks like a monkey. I then used to tell them that why don't you tell your children as to who our ancestors were. However I could only fight outside. At home I used to become depressed".

Mothers have to take the entire responsibility for looking after the disabled girl and the commitment is considered 'natural' for them. As stated by Shagufa Kapadia, "Excessive value is attached to traditional role and responsibilities, especially in the family context" (1999, p. 265). The responsibility for nurturance is thus shifted to women. In the case of disabled daughters, the care relationship gets linked to notions of self sacrifice thereby creating "a culture of female sacrifice" (Papanek, 1990, p. 173). The result is that women assume guilt when they are made to feel that their giving is lacking and put the blame squarely onto themselves. According to Hillyer (1993) the responsibility for treatment, and for advocacy, falls upon the mother whether by design or default. Instead of being credited for what she has done, for what the child is able to accomplish, the mother accepts responsibility for what has gone wrong.

As my informant Mrs. Varma shared, "I was told that it was all my negligence that was responsible for my child's disability. Mrs. Rastogi, whose daughter became retarded after having meningitis, was blamed by her in-laws for not having taken care of the child. Her experience became excruciatingly painful when her husband along with her in-laws blamed her for the child's condition. In the process she could not stop her father-in-law, who had T.B. from interacting with her daughter, resulting in worse condition of her daughter. She recounts her experience as she says, *"I think I must have not heard the doctors properly and made a mistake. It is really my fault"*. Such instances document the burden that the mother carries when she is held responsible for the child's diseases/impairments/disabilities. The father, however, is exonerated of all responsibility. Says Mrs. Sharma, "They just blame the mother for everything. Despite being educated, my in-laws continue to believe that the child had retardation, as there was a genetic defect within me. The question of my husband having it didn't arise". The consequence of this 'mother blaming' is that the mother can never get rid of the guilt, which adds on to her already fragile and vulnerable existence.

The mother-blaming scenario totally obscures the responsibility of society, which also plays a vital role in constructing the disability, particularly in relation to gender. The emotional scars that the mothers carry, as they are made to feel that they are responsible for the child's disability get reflected in the fears that exist regarding future pregnancies. Whereas in general, the mothers in India may undergo more pregnancies after a daughter, only to have a son, in case of a disabled daughter, this concern becomes secondary as the desire is now to have a 'normal child'. Thus the mothers themselves, become the carriers of societal oppression.

Of the twenty mothers interviewed, none had a second disabled child, though six of them did have normal children. Many of them had repeated abortions to avoid the birth of a "retarded child". It is thus clear that normality especially in contrast to developmental disabilities is definitely an attractive proposition. Mrs. Rastogi for instance had five abortions before having a normal girl child. The impact of such practices is dangerous both for the psychological and mental health of the mother, who undergoes this trauma.

> The fear of having another disabled child was apparent in Mrs. Duggal, whose second daughter was mentally retarded. On conceiving again, she decided to abort. She recalls her response,

"fear? You know those two months were simply hell for me. I couldn't sleep, couldn't lie down. All I could think was of how to get rid of the child".

The situation worsens for them, as within the family, there are suggestions of getting rid of the child even after she is born. As Mrs. Joshi recalls the horror of a visit from one of her own family member's, a paediatrician, who had come to condole.

> She came to condole and said, "Oh God! I am a doctor but I know that there is no hope for you and neither for your child. I don't want to say this but if... you withdraw feeding, the baby will fade away quietly and I know people who have done this. It's like a pact between parents and doctors. They do that in the hospital. In any case, you are taking her to the hill station. These babies are very weak, they catch a chill easily. Then pneumonia will not be far off, and you can let her go".

The experiential realities of these mothers thus again reinforces the belief that the disabled are better dead than alive. As I mentioned earlier in the chapter, this belief is concurrently linked with the promise that genetics represents the definitive elimination of prenatal impairment and disability. The stigma attached to disability makes the task of motherhood also extremely painful and difficult. The need of the mothers for a normal child, has to be understood in a cultural milieu, which produces a strong sense of shame in the mothers. They fight this guilt and shame by devoting their entire lives in looking after the disabled daughter, without ever questioning the 'naturalness' of this commitment. The guilt ridden mother often becomes harsh with other caregivers who are perceived as a 'failure' in this regard.

For most mothers, the mother who is unwilling to care for the developmentally disabled daughters is perceived as a 'cruel mother' who is 'selfish' and is shirking her responsibilities. This documents the general belief that motherhood is a natural role to which every mother must adapt. The argument thus, is, that if caring cannot come from mothers, no one else can be expected to take up that role. Such expectations do not take into account the fear and anxiety that are associated with disability.

Once again, feminists who have debated over the ethics of caring and the notion of equality (See Bhargavi Davar, 1999) have not taken note of the special conditions in which disabled, especially girls, are placed. Their focus on care has not included the mothers of disabled daughters. Within the realm of disability, the debates about ethics of caring have to be evaluated differently. The focus of the feminist discourse has not perceived the dangers in substituting the ethics of caring for ethics of equality, an unheard of dream for the caretakers and care receivers marked by disability.

Just as society fails to acknowledge the social identity and significance of disabled lives, even policy discourse is coloured by its biased orientation towards the notion of the 'perfect body'. The policies too are thus remiss in their neglect of women's issues related to disability as is reflected in the recent draft for a comprehensive National Policy for Empowerment of Women (Ministry of Women and Child Welfare). While it contains some groups of women, i.e. lower-caste, backward, minority, even though couched in 'welfare' terms, disabled women however do not find a mention in any of the categories highlighted as marginalised groups.

What is especially anguishing is that both Indian feminist thought and the women's movement fails to recognise that the problematization of women's issues applies equally to disabled women's issues. In principle, some disabled women might have benefited from the activities of certain women's groups, but there is no documentation of specific instances. On the other hand, there is ample evidence that disabled women are the victims of domestic violence and sexual violation (IFSHA: A report on women violence and mental health, 1999). There have been instances where, the national Indian media has included the story about a woman with cerebral palsy being abused by her father, or more recently a father killing his spastic daughter and then committing suicide. However, the invisibility of disability is so intense, that the ramifications of such disturbing news is never felt by the women's groups.

Further, Indian feminist scholars have not attempted to develop theoretical responses appropriate to the situation of disabled women. Very rarely have issues such as that of hysterectomy of the developmentally disabled girls been taken up for debate (Ghai, 2002c). Hysterectomy, an ethical proposition requires an engagement from women's groups as the practice from the vantage point of a disabled girl is oppressive, dehumanising, engendering and desexing. In fact, these practices are analogous to the ideologies of eugenics directed against minorities and those women who are perceived as deficient and barren.

It is not as if other issues have not been neglected within Indian feminist discourse. For instance, as Davar (Ibid) points out, mental health has not been a topic to which the feminist discourse has attended. Even she, fails to look at the issue of disability when addressing mental health. Research on mental health that is national in scope, omits discussion of women with disabilities. There is a presumption that their mental health issues will "obviously be different". This reflects the skewed attitude of mainstream feminists, who, while sensitively exploring distress as a major component, have once again excluded the disabled women from their agenda.

Even the Indian feminists who have done a lot of thoughtful work on the body have not considered the impaired body. As Niranjana points out, "Focus on the body has been a symbolic one where the body is perceived as sign or code important to the extent that it is speaking about a social reality other than itself. Suggestive as it may be to speak of the body as representing encoded social meanings, as an image of society or even a metaphor for society, the question remains whether these perspectives can acknowledge the materiality of bodies, not merely as they are formed/represented in a culture, but how they constitute the lived reality of persons" (Niranjana, 1998, p. 106). However, though this analysis takes up the issues of space and the female body, any mention of the disabled body is consistently omitted. Such omissions reflect the historical practices within a given culture that continue to render the disabled as invisible.

The exercise of charting out the concerns of disabled women in India however, is far from comprehensive, since factors such as poverty, caste, urban-rural divide further accentuate the problem. At this juncture, one might wonder as to what is so significant about these concerns, as many Indian women experience the same difficulties. My contention however is that, while the struggles might appear similar, they have to be understood in a disabling environment which is totally inaccessible and the negative societal attitudes which multiply the difficulties by taking the traditional as well as non-traditional choices away from the disabled women. Why this happens has been understood in terms of the 'Othering' process that the disabled go through, as they negotiate roles and spaces for themselves. I did make a brief mention about this process of alterity in the first chapter. I now elaborate on some of the work done in this area in terms of its implications for understanding disabled lives.

Alterity as a Process in the Invisibility of Disabled Women

The omission of the concerns of disabled women reflects an historical practice that continues to render them as invisible by engaging in the process of 'alterity'. The concept of alterity is sometimes a very palpable presence, while at other times only a significant trace in so far as it is implied in discussions of identity, domination and subordination, oppression, binary oppositions, and in claims made by a variety of social groups and movements (See Bill Hughes, 2000). For me, the work of Albert Memmi on *The colonizer and the colonized* (1967) serves as a useful benchmark in understanding the process of alterity. My reading of Memmi tells me that those of us who have been marginalised by our respective disabilities, enter the life space of the more complete "Other" from the position corresponding to that which the colonised holds in relation to the coloniser. Most fundamentally, my contention is that the creation of a devalued 'Other' is a necessary precondition for the creation of the able-bodied rational subject who is the all-pervasive agency that sets the terms of the dialogue. Taking over from the portrait that he draws of the 'Other' as it means to the coloniser, the colonised emerges as the image of everything that the coloniser is not. Every negative quality is projected onto her/him.

There are many significant aspects that need to be noticed in this description by Memmi. In fact they seem to be very familiar to many of us who share a disabled existence. First, the Other, is always seen as 'not', as 'lack', as 'void', as someone lacking in the valued qualities of the society, whatever those qualities may be. Second, the humanity of the other becomes 'indistinct'. Third, the Others are not seen as belonging to the human community, but rather as part of a muddled, confused, and nameless collectivity. They carry, according to Memmi, "the mark of the plural". In other words, they all look alike. This is indicative of the cultural hegemony that strives to posit an autonomous, rational and competent able-bodied subject as representative of a 'normal' existence.

It is with this assumption that the disabled as Memmi's colonised others, have heard on more than one occasion that they are "lacking". This internalised apprehension is affirmed by society, who continues to accept them as wanting and deficient. Further, the message of non-comprehension of their feelings and thoughts gets communicated. In fact whether they i.e. the Other, thinks or not, is doubtful. It is parallel to the traditional arguments about the rationality of women. It is quite strange that the colonised (in this case the disabled) must indeed be very odd, if she/he remains mysterious and opaque after years of living with the coloniser/able bodied society. This results in the Other being dehumanised to such a great extent, that all that she/he can become, is an object. Finally, in the world of the coloniser/non-disabled the ultimate desire is that, she/he should exist only as a function of the needs of the coloniser, that is, be transformed into a pure colonised. In other words, the existence is only as an object for himself or herself as well as for the coloniser/non-disabled.

The colonised loses its entity as a subject in its own right and remains only what the coloniser is not. It is thus an erasure both out of history and all significant aspects of development. At this juncture the coloniser asserts his fundamental immobility (Memmi, 1967). Confronted with this image, which is imposed on the disabled, who is cast as the Other he/she, like the colonised, cannot be indifferent to his picture. The ultimate result is that whatever image the coloniser has of the colonised is internalised by the disabled who is the colonised in this case. As Rose (1996) points out, "The injunction to be a particular sort of person is always bound up with an act of division: to be what one is, one must not be what one is not... the vicissitudes of identification are not ontological but historical and technical" (Rose, 1996, p. 309). It is in this context that Tom Shakespeare has used the concepts of 'otherness, anomaly and liminality' to critically examine the cultural representation and social exclusion of people with impairments. According to him, "Disabled people could also be regarded as Other, by virtue of their connection to nature; their visibility as evidence of the constraining body; and their status as constant members of mortality. If original sin, through the transgression of Eve, is concretised in the flesh of the women, then the flesh of the disabled people has historically... represented divine punishment for ancestral transgression. Furthermore, non disabled people define themselves as normal in opposition to disabled people who are not" (Shakespeare, 1997, p. 228). This indicates the negativity that is held in relation to the disabled. Though Memmi's work has not been very frequently used in understanding the disabled identity, in my view it can contribute substantially in understanding how there is always a distance between the coloniser and the colonised and by extrapolation, the disabled and the non-disabled.

This would be very familiar to the third world feminists, who have often complained of experiencing this process of Othering. In part it becomes possible because, as Chandra Mohanty points out, the speaking subject of feminist theory is always a western woman: "Third world women...never rise above the debilitating generality of the object status" (Mohanty, 1988, p. 80). In interpolating about, or speaking for the third world women, white western women seem to be colluding in the process of Othering, thus, reproducing oriental discourse in a feminist guise (V. Amos and Parmar, 1984).

In a similar vein Mary Daly's work *Gyn/Ecology: The metaethics of radical feminism* (1978) has been criticised for its embodiment of an orientalist discourse of the Hindu ritual of suttee (widow burning) by Joanna Liddle and Shirin Rai (1993). According to them, "All the sources used by her in constructing the history of *sati* in India and its justification, and acceptance by the Hindu culture, are western sources: furthermore, all except one are male. While Daly challenges the male version of cultural history, she does not do the same with the orientalist construction of a religion and people. Indeed she acquiesces in that construction and thus validates it" (Liddle and Rai pp. 17-18).

Edward Said (1978) is another scholar who recognises this process of alterity in his examination of the account of the European construction of the Orient. In emphasizing the political dimensions of this ideological move, Said understands the construction of the Orient as an outcome of a yearning for power. Orientalism, he states, is a Western Style for dominating, restructuring, and having authority over the Orient. He further argues that "European culture gained in strength and identity by setting itself off against the Orient as a sort of surrogate and even underground self" (Said, 1978, p. 3).

Nancy Harstock (1990) while referring to the work of Said comments that, "Interestingly enough, in the construction of these power relations, the Orient is often feminised. There is, however, the creation – out of this same process of the opposite of the colonised, the opposite of the Oriental, the opposite of women, of a being, who sees himself as located at the centre and possessed of all the qualities, values in his society" (Harstock, 1990, p. 161). Similarly, the disabled are framed as an opposition to the category of the able bodied or as pathological to the category of the normal. The way Orientalism is part of the European identity that defines 'us' versus the non-Europeans, the normal hegemony defines the disabled as the other within the Indian context.

Alterity, however has to be understood not as a given, but as a process which pushes a certain group of people to the margin of social worth, and constitutes as a threat to the social order and a challenge to the community. Yet, the paradox is that groups, which are considered as a threat, are also an integral part of society/community. The 'mainstream' is unable to identify itself or corroborate the elevated—at worst normal—nature of its being without reference to the margin. In fact a key feature of this process is that the notion of who and what others are. This includes knowledge of what they are like, what are their attributes and what sort of lives they lead. This knowledge is intimately related to 'our' notion of what and who we are. In other words, 'we' use the others to define ourselves. We understand ourselves in relation to what we are not.

One upshot of this understanding that the Other is a set of discourses through which the dominant group understands and defines itself, is that the Other is silenced and delegitimised. As Edward Sampson says:

> We know that the self needs the other in order to be a self at all. We know that when those selves are dominant in a given society, they can construct the other so as to affirm a particular kind of self for themselves... If I find myself in and through you, but no longer control the you that grants me my self, then I am forced to deal with a self which is beyond my control, and I may not enjoy this self with which I must now contend (Sampson, 1993, p. 153).

As disabled women confronting recurrent exclusion, we are not accorded expert status either on our lives or on that of the dominant group. Hegemony in this process of alterity does not take the form of a colossal and brutal domination. It just denies the disabled woman the authorship of her text or else to have her text dismissed as forbidden or incoherent. It is ironic that feminists who have engaged with the issue of difference, are united in their attempts to empower the powerless and have resolved to transform social inequalities, but have not picked upon the issues concerning the meaning of 'Othering' for disabled women. While the disability movement's failure to acknowledge disabled women can be fathomed as reflecting the patriarchal character of a society it accepts and aims to join, their disregard by the feminist movement, which claims objectivity through its theoretical deconstruction of oppressive social suppositions, is less understandable.

I feel that taking over from Memmi, Said and the third world feminists, the greatest contribution they can make is for an understanding of the process of alterity in disability studies.

Can this Exclusion be Understood?

Even though the recognition of differences is responsible for the emergence of at least a discourse on disability and gender, I cannot ignore the reality that it has not been able to affect much, if any change, either in increasing acceptance of disabled women's concerns in policy documents, or, in enhancing the quality of their lives. All it has managed to produce is a superficial acknowledgment of differences with an implicit assumption that the core issue is gender. The perceived need is therefore to raise the gender issues presumably adequate to address all women's lives regardless of their backgrounds and differences. What could be the reasons for the failure of feminists in the West as well as India to acknowledge and empathise with the existential realities of disabled women? Even though it is difficult to posit a clear answer to this query, I do attempt to analyse the reasons that seem significant. Also this query is rather complicated, as even within feminism rigid demarcations cannot be made between the developed world and the third world. For the present purpose, I first share some thoughts about feminism emanating from the west and then highlight the viewpoints of Indian feminists.

The first and foremost explanation lies in the stand point epistemology adopted in the 1970s, when the focus on the differences between men and women—combined with a clear sense of the magnitude of women's oppression—led to an elaboration of women's minds, as deeply shaped by the experience of oppression. The work of Nancy Chodorow and Carol Gillgan expressed the idea that women see the world differently than men. The seminal work following this approach is that of Nancy Harstock. Working on what she takes to be "the methodological base provided by Marxian theory, Harstock assumes a distinction between appearance and essence, circulation and production, abstract and concrete in which the "deeper level or essence both include and explains the surface" or appearance, and indicates the logic by means of which the appearance inverts and distorts the deeper reality" (Harstock, 1983, pp. 283-285). Considering the deeper level and comprehending the logic is possible only from a specific perspective, she argues, since "material life structures understanding" (Ibid, p. 287).

Thus whether one can see the reality of disability depends on where one is positioned. The vantage point for the non-disabled is the able-bodied normative ideal. Hartstock maintains that the sexual division of labour of patriarchy, similarly puts women in a fortunate position. While a woman's immersion in the world of use is a fact of her subjection, it is also the condition which enables her to see more clearly the deep reality of life. "The experience of continuity and relation- with others, with the natural world, of body and mind—provides an ontological base for developing a non-problematic social synthesis" (Ibid, p. 303). From this foundation, the reality of being a woman, emerges a feminist stand point, "a mediated rather than immediate understanding" (Ibid p. 288). Harstock thus conceives of women's experiences as providing the foundation for a liberatory vision.

Though Judith Butler agrees that there is some political necessity to speak as and for women, she questions the cost of reaching this unity. She says, "Surely that's the way in which the representational politics operate... and lobbying efforts are virtually impossible without recourse to identity politics. So we agree that demonstration and legislative efforts and radical movements need to make claims in the name of women" (Butler, 1992, p. 15). The goal of universal sisterhood has resulted in homogenising the very clear differences by resorting to certain core themes that are connected to women's lives. The very instant the category of women is invoked, as a universal constituency an internal questioning begins over the precise content of that term. All the same, the greatest strength of feminism has been the ability to be self critical and sensitive to the realisation that the implied homogeneity of the category of woman was working exactly in the same way as the patriarchal society. It is this realisation, which worked as a stepping-stone to a closer analysis of difference. Feminists, became particularly vigilant, in identifying the genuineness and authenticity of those who were presumably representing the cause of the other. This idea reached its epitome in the form of the questioning by contemporary feminism, of the category of woman throughout the world.

To quote Diane Elam, "I am suspicious of the universal particular, which the singular form, woman, forces us to consider, and likewise, I would not want to suggest that there is something that all women have in common. That would [return me] to a comfortable seat under the banner of "common oppression" (Elam, (1994, p. 32). The interest here is to understand the ways in which 'Women' is a permanently challenged site of meaning. The disabled women are but one such example of what it means to be a permanently challenged site of meaning. Thus, the struggle of the disabled women is not simply a struggle to assert an identity, but it is a fight to assert a difference and to account for the injustices done to women that have not found expression in the language of feminism. Even if disability does not play a role in the self-definition or 'lived experience' of the woman marked with disability, it does become the basis of most other people's definitions. This invisibility that disabled women experienced was partly due to a feminist rendering of history that followed an able-bodied story paradigm. This becomes clearly evident in Crosby's work (1991) where she offers a feminist analyses of history.

"To historicise is first to discover women where there had only been men, to see women in history, and to recognise a fundamental experience which unites all women, the experience of being the other... Such a reading obviously is no longer wholly within the discourse, which produces history as man's truth, no longer accepts history has only to do with men. Yet in a fundamental way this feminist reading is still within the space of formation of that discourse, for where once history revealed man's identity and fate as a finite being, now history reveals the truth of women's lives, the fate of being a woman, of being 'the Other'. The closed circle of recognition is still inscribed, for all women are women in the same way, and this discovery of identity is predicated on a whole series of exclusions.... A feminism that conceptualises women as a unitary category, which can be recognised in history, works within the circle of ideological reflection, guaranteeing that women will be found everywhere and will be similar" (Crosby, 1991, pp. 153-54).

Through the 1980s there was thus an increasing development of identity-based politics that raised this issue. Thus, politically, the concern with difference manifested itself in a more particularistic identity politics. This led to a generation of viewpoints in which the implicit understanding was that political action of any sort is impossible without a collective category asserting a definite identity. This identity then speaks from the vantage point of the specific marginalisation experience that has created the need for an assertion of that identity category. Identity politics was thus extremely powerful in creating a political currency. As a result, much important work was done on the specific oppressions associated with sexuality and race and within the Indian context, caste and religion. Although it is a fact that unity achieved at the cost of differences is unfair, it wasn't as if the universal category of woman has not contributed anything of significance to the cause of women. However along with these meta–narratives, what is needed is an examination of how these narratives determine women, so that a careful analysis of their inclusions and exclusions can take place. It is in this spirit that Denise Riley in *Am I that Name* emphasises that 'women' is an unstable category. According to Riley "the history of feminism has also been a struggle against overzealous identifications" of women (Riley, 1988, p. 5). However this uncertainty of women is no cause for bemoaning. In fact it is this uncertainty which makes feminism a viable political strategy.

Another reason for the invisibility of disabled women's concerns has been the mind set that is rooted in terms of binaries. When subjects are constructed as this one or the other, woman or man, dalit or Brahmin, black or white, non-disabled or disabled and so on. All binaries, according to Rutherford, "Operate in the same way as splitting and projection: the centre expels its anxieties, contradictions and irrationalities onto the subordinate term, filling it with the antithesis of its own identity; the other in its very alienness simply mirrors this and represents what is deeply familiar to the centre, but projected outside of itself. It is in these very processes and representations of marginality that the antagonisms and aversions, which are at the core of dominant discourses, and identities become manifest racism, and class contempt as the products of this frontier" (Rutherford, 1990, p. 22). Consequently the distance between the two categories never gets mapped out, thus leaving unexplored territories of human experience.

Reasons for Exclusion: An Indian Experience[3]

In the absence of any writings or dialogue related to the field of disability, I have taken recourse to some interviews that I conducted with active leaders in the field to get an insight into the reasons for this exclusion. In the following section, my aim is to share some of the reasons given by the feminists as well as the activists of the women's groups. However, before that, it is in order to consider the situation of the Indian women's movement, even though my effort will only scratch the surface of this subject.

The women's movement in India, according to Gandhi and Shah (1992) has no beginning or origin. "It has always existed as an emotion, as an anger deep within us, and has flowed like music in and out of our lives and consciousness and actions" (Gandhi and Shah, 1992, p. 15). As of today there are many streams within the movement which are ideological, class or community based, rural or urban based, and spread all over India. The movement evinces deep concern for what are conceived as basic societal issues. These include poverty, class and caste inequalities, labour related injustice, wages and employment, population technologies, sati (self immolation), dowry, female foeticide. With time, many other issues such as domestic violence, childhood sexual abuse, and sexuality have become dominant concerns of feminists for both theoreticians in the academy and activists in the women's movement. It is not difficult to locate critical discourses about all these issues both within the academy and practice. But it is also true that the emphasis of Indian feminism has not been on the individual but rather on the collective issues with significant political ramifications. Nonetheless, the feminist agenda in India, as in

---

[3]Some parts of this chapter have appeared in an earlier article, entitled "Disabled Women: An Excluded Agenda of Indian Feminism" *Hypatia*, 2002, 16(4), Fall: 34-52.

other countries, has focused on a reconfiguration of gender constructions in society by questioning patriarchal norms. This has focused action on programs aimed at recasting the traditional gender roles.

The common thread in this attempt to reinvent gender identities has been the experience of oppression shared by all women. Ironically, the movement's exhaustive list does not include disability oppression, despite the fact that disability cuts across all categories and may be associated with the experience of many of the other oppressions against which the women's movement is fighting. One reason highlighted by the theorists and activists alike has been that disabled women have not participated in the movement's meetings and actions. Consequently, neither accounts of their lives nor their challenges to feminist theory, have immediacy.

While this explanation may have some merit, it also underlines the inability of the feminist movement to consider what may prevent women with disabilities from actively participating in the movement's work. In a country where it is not unusual to develop structural amnesia with regard to a particular category of persons, there are few opportunities for disabled women to create an immediate presence and speak for themselves. The Other i.e. the disabled, is silenced because she *is* the 'Other', and the speech of the dominant group on her behalf reinscribes her Otherness simply through the fact of excluding her from the discourse. Yet, the feminist agenda, and the women's movement, have not remarked on these conditions. Possibly, the experience of disability is imagined to be opaque, intransitive, and idiosyncratic. In the absence of a sustained discourse about disability in Indian feminist theory, the mistaken belief that biological impairment prevents people from evolving as full social, psychological, political, aesthetic and cultural beings, continues to prevail. The impaired body thus becomes a source of exasperation, anguish, pain and torture. The prevalent ideals of the female bodies make it difficult for the women with disabilities to resist the dominant order and make it difficult if not impossible for them to identify with the phenomenon of aesthetisation. With the advent of consumerism, as Welsch puts it, "More and more elements of reality are being aesthetically mantled, and reality as a whole is coming to count increasingly on aesthetic construction to us. An array of goods and services are sold in the name of aesthetic practices. These are meant to normalise any body that is found to be deviating from the norm. It is only when a price tag is attached to those who do not quite fit the bill that problems start (Welsch, 1996, p. 1).

Another feature of the many interviews carried out by me was the recurrent use of disability as an analogue for other kinds of limitations. For example, one respondent stressed that "Being a woman is the biggest form of disability" (Kamala Bhasin, personal conversation). Another observed: "Disability is like belonging to the lowest caste possible" (Jaya Shrivastava, personal conversation). There are several ways of understanding these analogies. One option is to look at the socio-cultural meanings ascribed to female bodies and those assigned to disabled bodies. Both the female and the disabled body are excluded from full participation in public and economic spheres; both are conceived in opposition to a norm that is assumed to possess natural superiority. Such comparisons can be both emancipatory and oppressive. If the objective of invoking such comparisons is to understand different people's lived experience and grasp their authenticity, the potential is immense. However, if the underlying realities of the categories serve only at a metaphorical level, it can lead to a total erasure of the category, which is being invoked. It is true that analogy is a theoretical device that is meant to enable the move from more familiar to relatively unknown terrain in order to understand how a set of relations evident in one sphere might illuminate the other. However, if a comparison or the parallel pits one set of relations against the other, as is the case of women against disability, the strategic advantage of the analogy gets lost.

Without devaluing such metaphorical moves, I wish to focus on what gets 'valorised' and 'suppressed' in the process. My argument is that such analogising results in a suppression of the harsh reality of disabled women's lives, which are limited by conditions that are much more difficult than ordinary to transcend. A shift from the theoretical/ metaphorical to the material is essential to render visible the 'culture constructions' that have supported the currently flawed conceptualisations of disability and womanhood. In fact a careful analysis of such metaphors is required to unearth their meanings and functions, so that their power can be subverted. Till the popular refrain that being a woman is the biggest form of disability operates, the road to emancipation/empowerment is going to be a difficult one.

Nivedita Menon, an activist in the women's movement, and a political scientist by profession, feels that the invisibility of disability within feminism occurs because of mechanisms similar to those that have made women in general invisible in the larger society (Menon, 2002c). But as a feminist who feels disturbed by the neglect of disability issues, she thinks that the movement has the potential to grow and change. Another reason for the failure to represent women with disabilities is that within the Indian women's movement there are far too many issues and too few resources. Consequently, action has been oriented to the dramatic patterns which resonate in the lives of the majority of women who are able and normal, rather than to the minority who fail to exercise voice or agency.

While I have tried to separate the Indian and western scenario, in reality it is not an easy endeavour. I definitely do not wish to posit a "them and us" binary in the process, but at the same time I want to acknowledge that the specific cultural realities are different. The following chapter attempts to present the work that has emerged in the west.

3

Locating Disability in the Feminist Discourse: The Epistemic Contingency of the Disabled Feminists

In the previous chapter, I provided a glimpse of the reasons, which have resulted in the exclusion of the issue of disability from the feminist discourse in both the developed and developing world. As the developed world experienced the exclusion, there were many disabled feminists who responded to the challenge by providing a vision of an inclusive feminist project that takes into cognisance the issue of disability. In the present chapter, I share some of the ideas articulated in the west. I do this not because I offer solutions modelled on western thought, but to avoid re-inventing the wheel far too much. I am aware of the difference in the conditions of the developed and the developing worlds. All the same, I do wish to give my readers an idea of the nature of discourse that has emerged in the west. Obviously, within India, the cultural import would alter the nature of this discourse.

For many feminists in the west, who identified themselves as disabled, the disability has constituted their epistemic contingency. The latter term has had roots in multiple sources, but as Roof and Wiegman maintain, "Contemporary conversations about knowledge and the institution often focus on the way that academic discourse legitimises itself by disavowing the historical, cultural and corporeal specificity of its speaking. By exposing the way that objective and neutral methodologies repress the precise locations from which the speaker comes, academic discourses have begun to interrogate themselves from within, calling scholars to account, so to speak, for their own inescapable contingencies" (Roof and Wiegman, 1995, p. ix). Speaking from this epistemic contingency several disabled feminists have engaged with their own life experience to identify the specific oppressions faced by disabled women. I think the common thread has been their disappointment with feminist colleagues, which they have rightfully critiqued. Many times they have also lamented the neglect and expressed their despair. Similarly, the disability movement's male-centric attitude has been deplored. However, the very fact that these women endeavoured to raise a note of dissent, affirms their resistance to the twin hegemonies of patriarchy and normality.

The discourse that has developed has been at the interface of feminism and disability theories. The efforts include the works of Jenny Morris, Carol Thomas, Mairian Corker and Janet Price & Margrit Shildrick in Britain, Susan Wendell in Canada, Helen Meekosha in Australia, and, Rosemary Thomson in America to name a few. The list is definitely not exhaustive. However, since my aim is to share with the readers the different directions in the emerging discourse, an attempt is made to discuss their work in some detail. What is significant is that while each of them is deliberating with the issue of disability and feminism, the discourse that has developed is definitely not a unifying one, though commonalities are there. In this sense the debates about the unifying category of woman, within feminism, are reflected in the specific discussions of disability. The real test of any theory is its ability to reflect on stories and experiences. Though the origin of the authors that I share, is western, it is firmly grounded in the personal experiences of disability. Its theoretical capacity has enabled the disabled in the west to conceptualise their personal experiences within a broader framework. This knits together the personal and the political, the social and the intimate.

Jenny Morris

Jenny Morris has been possibly one of the most well known disabled feminists. She was one of the first to voice the dissent of the disabled women against the idea of 'double oppression' (patriarchy and normality). It is she who highlighted the neglect of the disabled women by mainstream feminists. She also underscored the gendered nature of disability studies and the disabled people's movement (See Morris 1991; 1993; 1996; 2001). Her major works include *Encounters with Strangers: Feminism and Disability* and *Pride against Prejudice: Transforming Attitudes to Disability.* According to her, "Disability research and theory either treats gender as invisible or separates the issue out into a focus on the experiences of disabled women. Thus, research often assumes the experience of disabled men to be representative of the disabled experience in general, and, when gender is introduced into the discussion, it is commonly in terms of disabled women experiencing a 'double disadvantage'. However, if we give full recognition to the importance of gender, the experience of both disabled men and disabled women will be more closely represented and explained" (Morris, 1993b, p. 85).

The exclusion of the disabled women's agenda from the mainstream disability politics is thus a serious issue for Morris. In arguing for an epistemic contingency, she calls for sharing of the personal experience of disability despite warnings by her male colleagues that it may imply a loss of the political voice. She asserts that the grounds on which a theory is judged is in relation to its validity for explaining experience. Though in several ways the feminist discourse still continues to ignore the disabled women, the attention that the disabled women have received, has a lot to do with Morris who sensitised feminists to include the issue of disability in their agenda. The disabled women who were/ are stereotyped as weak, pitiful, dependent and passive have been a marginalised voice. However, this cultural reading is often missing in feminist analysis. Morris points out this lacuna eloquently, "In the past, both non-disabled feminists and the men who dominate the disabled people's movement have been strangers to the concerns of disabled women. Our encounters with both groups have often made us feel powerless for we have either been traded as invisible or our experiences have been defined for" (Ibid, p. 1).

Emphasising the importance of asserting the disabled identity, Morris believes that "We are outraged that our voices are silenced so that our oppression is not recognised; we define as injustice to the exclusion of disabled people from mainstream society. In doing this we share with each other, and develop an understanding of, the detailed reality of our lives, using such politicisation of the personal to make sense of our experiences of prejudice and discrimination" (Ibid, p. 4). Further, she maintains that "We are often physically different from what is considered to be the norm, the average person ... Our bodies generally look and behave differently from most other people's bodies (even if we have an invisible physical [impairment] there is usually something about the way our bodies behave which reveals our difference from normal persons). It is not normal to have difficulty walking or to be unable to walk; it is not normal to be unable to see, to hear; it is not normal to be incontinent, to have fits, to experience extreme tiredness, to be in constant pain; it is not normal to have a limb or limbs missing. If we have a learning disability the way we interact with others usually reveals our difference. These are the types of intellectual and physical characteristics, which distinguish our experience from that of the majority of the population. They are all part of the human experience but they are not the norm; that is, most people at any one point in time do not experience them, although many may experience them" (Morris, 1991, p. 17).

Subscribing fully to an assertion of the disabled identity, Morris rejects any suggestions that reject the recognition of disability as an identity category. She reiterates the fact that though the self image of the disabled people is shaped by the non-disabled world's reactions, they have to resist the negative connotations attached to their lives.

While critical of feminism, it is the disability movement that Jenny Morris is most weary of. Her argument is that, claims to speak for 'disabled people' actually reflect the experience of disabled men thereby becoming a gendered articulation. Thus even within the same identity category, gender plays a significant role. A feminist reader will find an echo of the earlier struggles where men's experience were assumed to automatically represent the experiences of women. While emphasizing a re-writing of history Joan Scott says in her book *Gender and the Politics of History*, "Not the recounting of great deeds performed by women but the exposure of the often silent and hidden operations of gender that are nonetheless present and defining forces in the organisation of most societies. With this approach women's history critically confronts the politics of existing histories and inevitably begins the rewriting of history" (Scott, 1988, p. 27).

Morris in a similar vein points to a need of re-comprehending the disability movement to locate its gendered character. In her view the social construction itself implies that the experience of disability is inevitably a gendered one, and thus a different one for men and women. It follows that Morris also acknowledges that the experience of disability is also 'raced', 'classed', 'aged' and so forth. However I think what is missing in Morris's analysis is the recognition of the differences between the disabled women themselves. Though she is quick to reiterate the difference between the disabled and the non-disabled world, she appears to be homogenising the differences that exist between different categories of disabled women as well as other critical factors such as class, ethnic minority etc. Although she mentions them in passing, the recognition of differences between women is not posited very clearly.

From my vantage point of a third world disabled woman, Morris too, is treating disability as a unitary category. However, as part of the identity politics, her contributions are extremely relevant. She adds, "We can assert the importance of our experience for the whole of society, and insist on our rights to be integrated within our communities. However, it is important that we are explicit about the ways in which we are not like the non-disabled world. By claiming our own definitions of disability we can also take pride in our abnormality, our difference". (Morris, 1991, pp.16-17).

Morris does observe that most of our interactions are with people who are oblivious to our experiences. Consequently, the internalisations that the disabled women carry are necessarily prescribed by the non-disabled society. However to resist them, the disabled identity needs to be asserted fully to the isolation of other factors.

Susan Wendell

While Morris has undoubtedly contributed to the issue of disabled women, another feminist who has struck a note within the feminist world is Susan Wendell, a philosopher from Canada, who looks at the disabled woman as *The Rejected Body*. Wendell uses the terms "rejected body" and "negative body" to refer to those aspects of bodily life (such as illness, disability, weakness and dying), bodily appearance (usually deviations from the cultural ideals of the body), and bodily experience (including most forms of bodily suffering) that are dreaded, uncared for, reviled, and/or abandoned in a society and its culture (Wendell, 1996). According to her, though feminists have always criticised the idealization and objectification of women's bodies, recognising them as sources of exploitation and alienation; they have not taken disabled women within their purview. While focusing on ideals of appearance, grooming, and bodily demeanour for women, and on sexual and medical objectification of women's bodies, they have expressed their own body ideals, often insisting on women's strength and overlooking the fact that many women's bodies are not strong. While celebrating the bodily experience as a source of pleasure, satisfaction, and feelings of connection, there might be an underestimation of bodily frustration and suffering that bodily difference can produce and this needs to be recognised. As Wendell elaborates further, "Feminists have criticized and worked to undo men's control of women's bodies, without undermining the myth that women can control our own bodies" (Ibid, p.93). She substantiates her position by referring to Adrienne Rich, who wrote, "In order to live a fully human life we require not only control of our bodies (though control is a prerequisite); we must touch the unity and resonance of our physicality, our bond with the natural order, the corporeal ground of our intelligence". (Rich, 1976, 21).

Wendell underscores the fact that unless, "Feminists criticize our own body ideals and confront the weak, suffering, and uncontrollable body in our theorizing and practice, women with disabilities and illnesses are likely to feel that [that they] are embarrassments to feminism" (Wendell, 1996, p. 92). The experience that she shares is in the aftermath of nine months of living with the diagnosis of myalgic encephalomyelitis, popularly known as the chronic fatigue syndrome. It is significant to note that before the onset of the illness, Wendell had had a background of feminist theory by virtue of being part of the faculty of the women studies programme in Simon Fraser University in Canada. Thus it is both with the epistemic contingency of disability as well as her location as a woman, that she has understood the implications of disability. Conceiving disability as a social construction she observes, "The more I learned about other people's experiences of disability and reflected upon my own, the more connections I saw between feminist analyses of gender as socially constructed from biological differences between males and females, and my emerging understanding of disability as socially constructed from biological differences between disabled and the non disabled... It was clear to me that this knowledge [about living with bodily differences] did not inform theorising about the body by non disabled feminists and that feminist theory of body was consequently both incomplete and skewed towards healthy non-disabled experience" (Ibid, p. 5).

Wendell is different from Morris in the way she displays caution in using a universal category of people with disabilities. She notes that, "We now know from the extensive writings of women with disabilities that living with similar disabilities are different for males and females.

An emerging literature also reveals that living with similar disabilities is different for women of different races, classes, sexual identities and ethnicities" (Ibid, p. 70). She highlights the danger of over generalising from one disability to another disability, such as paraplegia from blindness.

Though Wendell is emphatic about disability providing an epistemic standpoint, she contends that, "Disability usually gives a person experiences of the world different from people without disabilities, and that being a woman with a disability usually gives a person different experiences from those of people who are not female and disabled, and that these different experiences create the possibility of different perspectives which have epistemic advantages with respect to certain issues. I do not claim that all people with disabilities, or all women with disabilities, have the same epistemic advantages, or that they all have the same interpretations of their experiences, or even that they have similar experiences. We are just beginning to investigate how much we have in common. ... I do want to claim that, collectively, we have accumulated a significant body of knowledge, with a different standpoint (or standpoints) from those without disabilities and that that knowledge, which has been ignored and repressed in non-disabled culture should be further developed and articulated" (Ibid, p. 73).

While critiquing the mainstream feminist work on the body, Wendell cautions that the criticism is to be distinguished from the approaches to cultural construction of 'the body'. These perspectives, according to her, confuse the lived reality of bodies with cultural discourse about bodies. Further, they deny or ignore bodily experience in favour of fascination with bodily representations. She maintains that, "I do not think my body is a cultural representation, although I recognise that my experience of it is both highly interpreted and very influenced by cultural (including medical) representations. Moreover, I think it would be cruel, as well as a distortion of people's lives, to erase or ignore the everyday, practical, experienced limitations of people's disabilities [restrictions of activity] simply because we recognise that human bodies and their varied conditions are both changeable and highly interpreted" (Ibid, p. 44).

What is significant from the point of view of a feminist discourse is her suggestion of incorporating age within the current definitions of disability. According to Wendell if age is recognised as a disability, our understanding that disability is not something other than ourselves, but is rather something which all of us will some day experience, will become better. She argues for the construction of a concept of humanity, which incorporates disability as a natural part of the human condition. An understanding that aging is disabling will assist the non-disabled people to see that disabled people are not the 'Other'. Says Wendell, "We need an understanding of disability and handicap that do not support a paradigm of humanity as young and healthy. Encouraging everyone to acknowledge, accommodate, and identify with a wide range of physical conditions is ultimately the road to self-acceptance as well as the road to increasing the opportunities of those who are disabled now" (Ibid, p. 18). She therefore reiterates the importance of a perspective, which is inclusive, so that the non-disabled can acknowledge the epistemic knowledge that the disabled possess. However, her belief that this understanding would augment and have the potential to change our thinking and our ways of life deeply does seem somewhat utopian. What remains significant is her view that disabled identity has to be kept alive to negotiate the political reality of disability.

Helen Meekosha

Helen Meekosha a scholar from Australia feels that, "While disability studies has begun to emerge as a potential location for the intellectual and political work that is required, the struggle to establish the area and the paradigms of the social model seems to have consigned the more complex theoretical questions of gender, ethnic and class relations to the margins" (Meekosha, 1998, p. 165).

According to her, "Some feminist scholars still appears hostile to the inclusion of disability within its frame of reference, as if the feminist project is being pushed one more step away from being able to speak with a strong political voice, particularly when the voice of the 'Other' is not recognizable" (Ibid, p. 166). She has also protested against the tendency of the use of the "language of disability" by feminist writers. By claiming that women are disabled by their capacity to reproduce or handicapped by their subordinate status in society, the feminist scholars have demonstrated the ignorance of the centrality of disability experience and its political ramifications. Says Meekosha, "Declaring female embodiment as a barrier to equal participation in society raises insurmountable problems and contradictions for disabled women" (Ibid,

p. 173). She cites Elijabeth Grosz, who in the opening sentence of her book *Volatile Bodies* (1994), argues that the body has been a conceptual 'blind spot' in contemporary feminist theory—blind being used as an adjective of condemnation. Feminism, which considers itself sensitive of the nuances of language, is not expected to use such labels unquestionably.

Taking up the issue of beauty pageants, Meekosha draws attention to the fact that a non-opposition to beauty contests and personality pageants has largely faded from the political agenda. This echoes in India too, as we witness the media and the general consumer culture valorising contests such as Ms. Universe and Ms. World. Fashion and beauty have become the new catchwords for both men and women. The understanding of earlier and more austere feminism, which recognised that these pageants represent a process of policing the female body, and are central to the oppression of women, are missing. For disabled women they add on to the already experienced sense of oppression. According to Meekosha, "Feminist thought can be useful to disability only when it starts questioning the unproblematized normal female body". While foreseeing the disadvantages of advocating "uncontrollable biology", Meekosha does not agree that a socially constructed disabled body can account for the entirety of the ordeal and sufferings of impairment, specially the subjective experience.

While I take up some parts of her debate in the next chapter, it would perhaps suffice to say that, disability theorists, following feminism's rejection of biology as the determining factor in the making of the gendered or racialized body, have similarly rejected biology as the determining factor in the making of the disabled body. They have questioned the dominance of the medical and rehabilitation paradigms, which seek to transform and normalize, indeed 'cure' the disabled body. Their argument that the disability/ability dichotomy as grounded in biological functioning or lack of functioning, is fallacious, has been a significant political and theoretical advance. But social constructionists of disability tend to assume a fixed and permanent disabling state. This approach does not take into account many disabilities, which are progressively degenerative, thus changing the body identity in numerous ways at different times. The disabled women therefore need to continuously renegotiate the relationships between the body, self and the socially constructed disability.

Meekosha lays stress on the understanding of the process of disabled embodiment only within the historical, cultural and class contexts. If the body is a site of political struggle, disabled women are involved in multiple contests, which may result in unexpected alliances with dispossessed Others. Meekosha highlights some of the issues that are involved in the feminist rendering of the issues of disabled women. She points out to the necessity of attending to first the academy in which, the struggle to position disabled bodily experiences within feminist discourses must be recognised. Secondly, disabled women should not be perceived as passive recipients but rather agents in their own right who despite the severely medicalised and normalised selves fight on both ideological and material terrains. The demand is for a right to womanhood and a bodily status beyond that of burden, so that no desire is deemed as an attempt to normalise a pathological body. Finally, she calls for a feminist interrogation of science, technology and medicine so that interconnections between gender, bodies and disability can be understood.

According to Meekosha, any feminist understanding of the disabled women which restricts itself to the discussions of the Welfare State and the role of women as care takers, cannot become inclusive. Further, no serious attention has been given to the 'cared-for' who is regarded as genderless. In addition there is objectification leading to the cared for becoming the Other for the carer. Disabled women in Meekosha's analysis, are included under common 'cared-for' in this debate, assumed as part of the barrier that contributes to women's secondary or privatised status. Even when a feminist analysis has been undertaken by Hillyer, in her book *Disability and Feminism* (1993), it has not considered the critical relationship between the female carer and the disabled woman. Hillyer's analysis fills a very crucial gap as it underscores the vital importance of including disability in the caring research. However, the issues of caring and autonomy from the perspective of disabled women remain untouched. The feminist project therefore, needs to do a careful analysis of the ethics of caring in the context of the disabled women. A certain caution has to be exercised in contextualising caring within the parameters of justice, as the connotations of a disabled existence might demand interdependence, and, not full autonomy.

Carol Thomas

A more recent work by Carol Thomas (1999) entitled, *Female Forms* endorses a materialist feminist conception of disability. In Thomas's view, a materialist has the potential to best explain how the social relationships which constitute disability are generated and sustained within particular social and cultural formations. All the same, she does underscore the fact that a materialist conception of disability must be informed by feminist perspectives, because disability as other domains of life is always gendered.

Thomas points out, in particular, that an understanding of disability which does not question the untold ways that socio-cultural processes and practices generate negative and blinkered notions about disabled people, fails to account for the fact that these discursive practices often have detrimental effects on the respective quality of the well being of disabled individuals. Thus in a theoretical gesture designed to close this gap in a social model, Thomas offers an alternative, an extended understanding of disability. This understanding defines disability as 'a form of social oppression involving the social imposition of restrictions of activity on people with impairments and the socially engendered undermining of their psycho-emotional well being' (Thomas, 1999, p. 3). Although, 'restriction of activity' emphasised by the social model approach is understandable, the meaning of disability has to be understood in a much broader framework.

The background of Thomas's formulation lies in the Fundamental Principles of Disability proposed by Union of Physically Impaired Against Segregation (UPIAS, 1976). The principles were concerned with the barriers, to the full participation in the labour market and the independent living, which people with physical impairments confront. From this initial emphasis on economic concerns and independent living which people with physical impairments confront, she notes, the reformulation of disability in the social model has enabled other socio-structural barriers (e.g. in the built environment, to equal educational opportunities and to full participation in civic and political processes), to be brought into relief (Ibid, pp. 16-17). Though Thomas acknowledges that the social model does not sense the interests of people with particular forms of impairment (for instance, deafness, learning difficulty and mental illness), whose experiences and needs do not 'fit' with it (Ibid, pp. 23-25). Notwithstanding such criticisms Thomas maintains, those cultural processes and practices can be fully incorporated into materialist social model approaches (Ibid, p. 60). However, she proposes a social relational understanding of disability so that it includes both the structural issues as well as the psycho-emotional aspects of disability. The psychological and emotional issues are extremely significant, as even if there was an absence of structural disability in the society, impairment per se can debilitate the strength of disabled women. According to Thomas, materialist social model approaches can account for the psycho-emotional dimensions of disablism, which are closely associated with these processes and practices. As she explains it, a materialist feminist conception of disability, which takes account of personal experience, would recognise that the psycho-emotional effects of disablism, 'are just as much a part of disability as are "restrictions of activity" in domains such as employment, housing, and independent living' (Ibid, p. 60).

My contention is that an appropriate socio-political definition of disability would identify cultural processes and practices as on par with restrictions of activity. For although Thomas argues that the psycho-emotional effects of cultural processes and practices can be just as disabling as limitations of activity and, hence, should be accounted for in a socio-political definition of disability, she does not suggest that the cultural processes and practices themselves can be just as disabling as restrictions of activity and should be taken into account in such a definition.

Yet, I would argue that in a developing country like India, it will be appropriate to understand disability from a materialist framework, the cultural meaning of disability would have to be understood in a much more concerted fashion. As Shelley Tremain puts it, "It is precisely cultural phenomena such as hegemonic epistemic regimes, regulatory discursive practices and exclusionary dialogic mechanisms which disable some of the very populations, which feel marginalized by and excluded from the [social] model" (Tremain, 2000, p. 827). Further, this understanding might be more valid for disabled women with physical impairments. However, it does not do justice to the modes of oppression that people with, for instance, sensory and cognitive impairments confront. As Tremain points out further, "the epistemic practices and regimes which de-legitimise, invalidate, and discredit constituents of the latter population [people with sensory and cognitive impairments] as subjects, that is, producers of knowledge" (Ibid). Such practices can neither be included into a notion of constraints of activity, nor can they be termed as the psycho-emotional effects of these limitations. Hence, caution needs to be exercised so that the specific impact of different impairments can be charted out individually. Thus the disability theory would be enriched if it were to follow the second wave feminism in questioning the universal category of impairment or disability.

The emerging discourse is indicative of the fact that insofar as disability theorists and researchers have assumed that the definition of disability propounded by UPIAS is a comprehensive one, they have committed an error analogous to one made by the white, heterosexual middle-class feminists who dominated early second-wave feminism in Europe and north America. For these feminists, 'gender' signified the asymmetrical relationships between 'women' and men', and 'women's oppression' was constituted in their difference from men. The assumption thus was that, the experiences of black women, women of colour, lesbians, poor women and working-class women could be simply included into the predicted notions of 'women' and 'women's oppression', which they had formulated on the basis of their own experiences. However, currently most feminists have come to acknowledge that a more politically and theoretically astute feminism would identify the ways that gender is inextricably intertwined with other axes of power. That is, the category 'women', should be investigated and re-explored along race, class, caste, and developed/ developing world contexts. A number of the foundational concepts of both feminism and disability theories would then get re-examined, eliminating some of the exclusionary aspects of both these discourses.

Rosemarie Garland Thomson

Thomson, a theorist from America, examines disability in the context of feminism's insistence that standpoint shapes politics; that identity, subjectivity, are cultural constructs to be questioned; and that all representation is political. Demonstrating the contributions which literary criticism can make to disability studies, her focus in her book *Extraordinary Bodies* is on disabled women. She writes, "To denaturalise the cultural encoding of these extraordinary bodies, I go beyond assailing stereotypes to interrogate the conventions of representation and unravel the complexities of identity production within social narratives of bodily differences" (Thomson, 1997, p. 5). In this project, she draws heavily on contemporary literary and feminist theory, in casting light on the construction of normality, by examining how corporeal deviance is a consequence of cultural rules' about what is understood as able-bodiedness. According to her, "Constructed as the embodiment of corporeal insufficiency and deviance, the physically disabled body becomes a repository for social anxieties about such troubling concerns as vulnerability, control and identity" (Ibid, p. 6).

Thomson's work offers an 'academic' perspective on disabling representation, although her book is also intended as a political intervention in regarding disabled people as akin to a minority ethnic group. She advocates, "A universalised disability discourse" that draws on feminism's confrontation with the gender system requires understanding the body as a cultural text that is interpreted, inscribed with meaning—indeed—made within social relations" (Ibid, p. 22). This would establish disability as a difference rather than lack. However, she does this within a background in which she takes up the disability as pathological in contrast to the normate which according to her is a "neologism which names the veiled position of the cultural self, the figure, outlined by the array of deviant Others, whose marked bodies shore up the normate's boundaries" (Ibid, p. 8). According to her, normate is that identity who by virtue of the bodily configuration and cultural capital can become a position of powerful authority. Such a de-constructed reading in Thomson's view, reveals a very narrowly defined profile, describing only a minority of actual people. Conceiving disability at the interface of both bodily inadequacy and the deficit environment, she calls for feminism to recognise disability, as a formal identity category so that physical differences can be accepted more readily, or, ordered into a hierarchy. She does not visualise any political advantage in writing off the category of disability in accordance with the poststructuralist critique of identity, in the way that some feminists have argued for abandoning the concept of woman as hopelessly imprisoning and abstract" (Ibid, p. 23).

While she analyses impaired bodies as extraordinary, her emphasis is on the individual body, rather than the structural and collective forces. In this sense, she comes very close to accepting body as the site for struggle. She says, "The strands of feminist thought most

Locating Disability in the Feminist Discourse

applicable to disability studies are those that go beyond a narrow focus on gender alone to undertake a broad socio-political critique of systemic, inequitable power relations based on social categories grounded in the body. Feminism, for Thomson, is thus a theoretical perspective and methodology that examines gender as a discursive, ideological, and material category which interacts with but does not subordinate other social identities or the particularities of embodiment, history, and location that inform subjectivity" (Ibid, p. 21). According to her even though the methodology is complex, the feminist objective of the need to rewriting the category of woman with political significance should necessitate a critical engagement with disability.

She insists that the disabled body must resist interpretations of certain bodily configurations and functioning as deviant and problematise the ways in which differences are invested with meaning. She sees a distinct similarity between feminism and disability studies, as both seek to scrutinise the enforcement of universalising norms, cross-examine the politics of appearance, delve into the politics of naming and create positive identities. She sees both femininity and disability as inextricably caught in patriarchal culture, as Aristotle's equation of women with disabled men exemplifies. States Thomson, "Not only has the female body been labelled deviant, but also historically the practices of femininity have configured female bodies similarly to disability. However, society has remained oblivious to the physically disabling effects of practices such as foot binding, scarification, clitoridectomy, and corseting which were (and are) socially accepted (Ibid, p. 27). A feminist project for disabled women needs, then, to focus at times on the variations in the body, and at the same time, to question the identity it supports. A feminist disability politics would espouse the right for women to define their physical differences, and their femininity for themselves, rather than conforming to accepted understanding of their bodies.

She however critiques the feminist expectation of autonomy and independence as these goals undermine disabled women's struggle. According to Thomson, "By tacitly incorporating the liberal premise that levels individual characteristics to posit an abstract, disembodied subject of democracy, feminist practice often leaves no space for the needs and accommodations that disabled women's bodies require"(Ibid, p. 26). She cites the case of a well-known disability rights activist Judy Heumann's anger and frustration with some white feminists, "When I come into a room full of feminists, all they see is a wheelchair. These conflicts testify that feminists—like everyone else, including disabled people themselves—have absorbed cultural stereotypes. Further she focuses on the fact that the disciplinary regimes of feminine beauty such as cosmetic surgery, often mask the apparently obvious categories of the normal and the pathological. The surgical procedures are intended to improve the appearance of women's bodies which are considered as unmodified, as un-natural and abnormal. The alteration is needed so that the bodies can appear as normal and natural. While Thomson's theorising evoked a considerable degree of interest in the re-conceptualisation of extraordinary bodies, she has not escaped criticisms which come from disabled feminists, who question the hierarchy of disability, where the visually recognisable categories are valourised. One of the very vocal critics has been Corker. I share Corker's viewpoint in the following section.

Mairian Corker

Corker has problems with Thompson's construction of disabled bodies as extraordinary rather than as deviant. While appreciative of her attempt to shift the conception of disability from pathology to (positive) identity, Corker is critical of what she perceives as the ubiquitous fleshy concerns of feminist philosophy and social theory. In her view, "Thomson's standpoint politics foregrounds visible disabilities and freakery" (Corker, 2001, p. 37). However, these attempts according to Mairian Corker are problematic as they construe 'identity' largely in terms of recognition. They also represent endeavours which understand 'identity', as located at the peripheral level. Mairian Corker thus questions the assumption that the asserting and honouring of physical symbols of uniqueness as 'identity' is less worrying than the notion of impairment as natural and "given".

Corker begins by reiterating the fact that, even though there has been an attempt on the part of the feminists to recognise the importance of social and cultural diversity among and within women. However, this recognition of difference, both in theory and practice, obliterates the experience of disabled women, whose difference is understood in purely biological terms. She underscores the fact that within the feminist discourse, disability is invisible or at best as an add-on category. She emphasises that both the feminist discourse as well as the disability theory must take account of the significance of including the disabled women's experiences into the theoretical discourse. From the vantage point of a third world disability activist to a feminist, Corker has made two significant contributions in enunciating the understanding of disability. First, what is really meaningful is her caution about the dangers of applying a universalised disability discourse, which both implicitly and explicitly assumes a certain uniformity in the material conditions of disabled all over the world. Given the inequalities between the developed world and the developing world, this assumption can result in the negation of the widespread conditions of poverty, which exacerbates the experience of disability.

In a country like India, where the majority lack access to even the basic necessities, the assumption of universalised conditions has absolutely no meaning. Social and cultural diversity add on to the differences that exist between the developing, or the majority world—to use Emma Stone's terminology (1999) and the developed world.

I (the author) agree with Corker's point, that like the disabled throughout the world, disabled in India too, are the most marginalised groups in society. Says Mairian Corker, "The disabled are relegated to the bottom of the hierarchy of the oppressed in social systems built on structural inequality" (Corker, 2001, p. 36). Since feminism has always challenged the structural system of gender, it is seen as an objective perspective, which can question such inequities. Both within the disability studies as well as feminism, assertion of specific identities such as disabled and black is considered essential to confront the prejudice that produces clichéd versions of people such as disabled. However, there is some merit in Corker's suggestion that, in any system which is recognized as pluralist, the only identities that can make a dent in that plurality are those that can match within the overall logic that approves and controls the consensus. In Mairian Corker's words, "The regulative power of universalising discourse constitutes minoritizing expressions of difference" (Ibid, p.37). Consequently her apprehension of falling into the epistemic trap of universal "truths" is extremely valid.

Second, which in my understanding seems to be both a critical and debatable feature in Corker's analysis is, her perception of an implicit assumption of the disability theories, which believe and reinforce the domination of particular disabilities. Arguing that the various disabilities cannot be weighed in the same scale, she calls for an introspection of the existing critiques of 'normativism' within disability studies. The latter is based on certain assumptions which are carried over from ablest hegemony. Conceptualising the different disabilities in an uniform fashion can be as oppressive as the patriarchal or ablest hegemony. She thus raises a crucial issue by critiquing the homogenisation of disability. This has resulted in a reification of the disabled identity and reduced it to particular kinds of impairments—physical, mental, irreversible, tangible and severe types, in a way that can dissuade many people from adopting a disabled identity and participating in a community of disability. The disability theory even with a social vantage point may harbour its own set of indigenous essentialisms and exclusions. However, in my view, the solution is not to surrender to these essentialisms and exclusions, but to work towards a more inclusive approach. This will make Mairian Corker's point about manoeuvring the social world being an altogether different and more complex cognitive task, than manoeuvring one's way around the physical material world, more understandable. While it is possible to render assistance for mapping the physical territories, it is impossible to have a instruction booklet for the social world.

Taking her own experience of struggling to make meaning in the context of an embodied uncertainty and volatility, that is characteristic of deafness as communicative difference in a hearing-speaking world, Corker is critical of social practices that are legitimated by the dominant hearing-speaking culture. She illustrates this by sharing how the practice of "discussing" (used extensively by the hearing-speaking world) becomes repressive and harsh for her as she can only function, with the assistance of a third party who has the role of translating. However, this translation can never be fully objective as the translator by default introduces his/her own cultural milieu in both the directions. Corker reifies this point by quoting bell hooks' who maintains that 'discussion' in the hearing-speaking way represents "an absence of choices" (Hooks, 1984, p. 5). Anita Silvers, while agreeing with Corker's portrayal of the domination of speech in the experience of deaf and hearing people, points out that this difference does not imply that deaf and hearing people give different meanings to 'discussion', any more than when Corker (who is Deaf)[1] and Silver (who is mobility impaired) mean different things by the term "downstairs" (Silvers, 1998). Silvers's experience of coming down the stairs in a power wheelchair is sure to be very different from Corker's experience of a graceful, elegant and surefooted descent.

For me in a developing world, where architectural barriers are more a norm than exception, neither physical nor social navigation is an easy endeavour. If there has to be an attempt to initiate a universalised discourse, the hierarchies of accessibilities within the developing and the developed world have to be recognised. In a scenario, where, the non availability of assertive devices such as power wheel chairs or visual/hearing aids are questionable, Corker's contention that accommodative outcomes, such as building ramps for those who use wheelchairs is not the same as providing bilingual education and sign language interpretation for those who are deaf becomes only partially right. While I agree that the social environment can never be rendered immutable in a way that accomplishes the disappearance of sensory disability, I do not think that cultural meaning attached to any disability can be erased even if it was possible to change the living conditions that lessen the limitations experienced by them.

Notwithstanding my reservations about Corker's suggestions, I do wish to submit that her attempts in introducing sensibility in the disability discourse is laudable. 'Sensibility', according to Corker, does not imply only the act of perception. "It actually refers to set of individual or collective dispositions to emotions, attitudes, and feelings that are relevant to value theory, including ethics, aesthetics, and politics. Sensibility however, undoubtedly incorporates the subjective aspect of perception that philosophers call sensation, and thus, I would argue, it troubles particular understandings of our access to a fixed mental or physical reality" (Corker, 2001, p. 41). Sensibility thus prompts ways of being in and knowing our world that is, "materialized in contradictory bodies in process, and performed in shifting aesthetic, ethical, and political values" (Ibid, p. 41).

As Donna Haraway indicates in her widely acclaimed book *Situated Knowledge* (1988), sensation and sensibility are not located

---

[1] D is capitalised to denote a category of hearing impaired people, who construct themselves as belonging to an ethnic minority with a different language.

at the apparent level of reception and elucidation of 'reality', but are active processes that are the product of social and historical forces. Within the purview of Corker's analysis, an understanding of identity that privileges the present and the visible, endangers a disembodiment of sensibility specially if it assumes that sensation is a direct line to 'reality' and 'truth'. Therefore, sensibility must be re-articulated in order to dodge the essentialist thinking inherent in postulating a fixed identity implicit in accounts of cultural diversity. This will enable a dialogue across difference in ways that dislodge disability from its position of negativity in feminist thought. She points out to the contributions made by biological conditions such as deafness and blindness to an understanding of the lived experience. What is significant to understand is that within their social world there is a possibility of comprehending meaning at the level of sense that in many ways determines the degree of mutuality that can be reached in social interaction. Further, social meaning must be assumed and illustrated within cultural contexts often radically different from our own. To quote Corker, "Social languages are not parcelled out in rationally consistent conceptual schemes they overlap, interact, fuse, form, and are deformed" (Corker, 2001, p. 40). Therefore, the combination of 'physical or mental impairment' — a dualism that is also employed in the disability discourse seems indefensible. A mere addition of the term sensory does not change its underlying pattern of significations. "The sensorially impaired is always in a state of dys-appearance" (Ibid) because the division between normal and disabled remains undivided. Thus caution needs to be exercised in equating the physical and social.

The fact that those disabled people who seem to be arriving at such a rational consensus may themselves have negative attitudes about impairment, and limited knowledge in respect of people with impairments dissimilar to their own (French, 1993), needs to be remembered. Since much of this experience is constituted in and through social interaction, an exploration of these embodiments not as adjuncts to the physical disability but as an endeavour to create an inclusive society is important. This can be achieved only with the development of responsible and responsive ways, or 'sensed' ways, of thinking collectively that can be used to balance the political project of emancipation from oppression.

Another contribution of Corker is to question the tendency of disvaluing disability. The feminist accounts that attempt to transform pathology into identity, without challenging the theoretical framework of binary thought, seem to regard impairment as inherently disvaluable. As Corker states, "Reading 'the monstrous body' as a cultural text avoids consideration of whether it has or can have intrinsic value, because, in this account, value is always socially constructed, and, I would argue, 'easily' (though not necessarily simply) read". In attempting to state "the norm" of monstrosity, which I think is what is meant when these accounts refer to 'claiming' disability—but without making it valuable—incommensurability and normativism are reproduced, which creates "other" absences and other "injustices"(Corker, 2001, p. 46). Those of us who have lived with disabilities have gained immensely about the fragile boundaries that exist between normality and abnormality. Thus, if disability is to be understood as a deviation from some pre-stated standard, and inherently valueless then there is some benefit in understanding the position of Price and Shildrick (1998) who state, "All those things which must be excluded from the normative binary of self and other, which must be silenced and forgotten, may acquire in their dislocation an accumulative force that returns to inhabit the moments of fracture" (Price and Shildrick, 1998, p. 201). In other words, it is important to comprehend that both the deaf people as well as blind people make sense of their world through the ensuing forces of vision and audition respectively. There is, in fact, no possibility of examining the mutual constitution of deafness and blindness without arresting the binaries of presence/absence or positive value/negative value that cancel out. Similarly, the resolution of the debates arising from the different understanding of "discussion" and "downstairs" within differing ontological frameworks is situated in raising queries about the association between specific and universal, centralised and decentralised, local and global, individual and collective, and rights and accountability.

A dedicated and mature collective vision, while it might derive from a specific focus, has to posit disability as not being inherently valueless. Corker sees this happening if disability can be 'sensed', and by adopting an affirmative course of action. However, the disability narratives will be more meaningfully understood, if there is a possibility of an open dialogue across differences both at the apparent as well as at the 'deep' level of implication without predetermining the nature of the possibilities that can be realized. A disability theory that restricts the meaning of disability in its own set of presumptions will end up setting exclusionary standards, thus setting a hegemony within a counter-hegemony that it stands for. The room for dissent which is essential for any reflective theorising would then be lost.

Janet Price and Margrit Shildrick take an approach closer to the postmodernist theory and raise some significant questions for the disability theory. Price, a feminist, has the background of living with a diagnosis of myalgic encephalomyelities. Their call is for "new approaches that suggests both a revaluation of existing concepts and a reordering of binary hierarchies, such as ability/disability, health/disease, and normal/abnormal. More challenging yet is the opportunity to set out innovative points of departure that go beyond the rearrangement of scholarship around a given materiality—the disabled body—to contest the very notion of any such fixed object of concern and, to open up the issue of uncertainty and vulnerability, as that must suggest to us the possibility of a re-conceived ethics" (Price and Shildrick, 1998, p. 224).

My attempt in this chapter has been to provide a slice of the issues that have been picked up and debated by the western feminists, as an exhaustive review is beyond the scope of the present endeavour. Nevertheless, the viewpoints that I have shared do point out that for a feminist orientation regarding disability, the questions of impaired body are significant. While the importance of bringing about structural and economic changes cannot be undermined, the issues related to the body are equally critical. Finally what emerges rather clearly is that to arrive at a consensus on whether the disability discourse and activism would be enriched by an assertion of an essential disabled identity is a difficult question, as the issues in claiming this identity are complex and varied. It would be futile to argue against giving up of the experiential reality, as this reality becomes a benchmark to share both similarities and differences. However, it would be pertinent to recognise that this reality can never move beyond the discursive realm as well as politics of its constitution. Therefore the issues of power, discourse and (con)text in the construction and use of the term 'disabled' assume a great importance. In the next chapter I turn to two major unresolved issues.

4

Some Unresolved Issues

Social reality exists, so as to speak, twice, in things and in minds, in fields and in habitus, outside and inside of agents. And when habitus encounters a social world of which it is a product, it is like a fish in the water: it does not feel the weight of water, and it takes the world about itself for granted.

Bourdieu and Wacquant (1992, p. 127).

Having shared the viewpoints of the feminists who are disabled, I now wish to highlight how in making disability a special condition, several pertinent issues have been overlooked. There is a tendency to dichotomise impairment and disability. Consequently, theorising of the impaired body has remained contentious. Moreover, the discourse continues to deal with the paradox of identity politics. I take up both these issues in this chapter and in doing so reiterate, that had the feminist rendering of disability avoided the label 'special' or 'doubly oppressed', it would not have had to face the accusation that issues connected with the lives of disabled women have been excluded. As will become clear, both the issues connected to body and the political movements, which rely on identity based tools, are very close to the feminist heart. That these issues are equally significant and problematic for both disability discourse and feminism make it clear that they are not mutually exclusive. All the same let me admit that there are no easy solutions. My intention is to expose the tensions inherent in understanding both the body and identity in the context of disability. I do this with an implicit and explicit hope, that I would be able to establish, if not sisterhood, at least commonality with the wider feminist discourse and the male-centric disability movement.

The Disabled Body: Impairment versus Disability

Fat bodies, thin bodies, male bodies, female bodies, young bodies, old bodies, shaped bodies, beautiful bodies, broken bodies, dark bodies, fair bodies, fit bodies and diseased bodies. The last decade has seen an explosion of theoretical speculation about the body, which has focused both on showing the primacy of the biological body, as well as contending that the body is a social construct. Historically, both within disciplines such as psychology in which I have received my basic training, and other allied fields such as sociology, the relationship between mind and body have been the focus for years. The crux of the debates has revolved around the question of the supremacy of mind over body.

The feminist inquiry has found these debates both intriguing as well as problematic. It is difficult to locate any feminist discourse that proceeds without understanding the body/bodies at some point of time or the other. Though the vantage point of such inquiries has varied, most of them have been troubled by the well-known Cartesian divide of mind and body, in view of its significant implications for their own lives. Feminists, thus, have always been sensitive and concerned with the nature of the discourse on the body, which seems to have covered diverse issues such as reproduction, sexuality, violence to name a few. Historically, the task of the feminist movement was to challenge the traditional perception of women's bodies as subordinate.

In the earlier part of the political struggles both in India, and in the west, the belief that biology is destiny was contested. The contest led to the realization that all bodies carry cultural and social inscriptions. Therefore, the conclusion that the specific cultural forms establish the pattern of the body both when it is considered perfect as well as ill. Conceived in this way, the body has been forced to vacate its residence on the nature side of the nature-culture duality and take up residence within culture (Susan Bordo, 1993, p. 33). Notwithstanding the essentialist nature of these arguments there was a proliferation of research that was aimed at proving the thesis that body is more a central metaphor for society rather than corporeality.

Within the Indian scenario, the notion that the body is the site for ideological contestations appears with reference to many issues such as partition (Das, 1991), embodiment (Meenakshi Thapan, 1998), space (Niranjanana, 1998), to name just a few. The emerging discourse, critiqued the patriarchal interests underlying these crucial aspects of the human experience and covered a lot of political ground in an attempt to fight the use of the female body as a site for ideological contestation. Despite these attempts, the notion of embodiment has remained contentious within feminist theory/discussion.

The apprehensions in acknowledging the centrality of the corporeal are perceived as diminishing the claim to full equality. Consequently, the pre-given, biological, sexed body which is open to mediation, and consequent change by social processes has been accepted. Thus, the biological body either disappears as in cyber literature or, it lives with the perception that biology is synonymous with mechanism and fixity. In this sense, attention has focused more on the socially constructed body—the malleable surface of an internally stable corporeality. In other words, though the body is influenced by the discourse, there is very little known of the opposite i.e. how the body reacts and affects the discourse.

Mostly scholars have tended to ignore the fact that human beings, and women more than men, are embodied beings who very often utilize their bodies as a means of organising insights regarding the circumstances surrounding them. What becomes clear in this discourse is that, it is not our bodies per se which write the story, rather, it is the way in which society constructs our bodies which is instrumental to the understanding of the body. Mary Douglas, the well known feminist, has talked at length on the ways in which bodies occupy an ambivalent space and are socially 'policed' for leakages and crossings between outside and inside spaces. The body according to her is also implicated as "a vehicle of communication, that informs the recent theory, contesting the notion of communication as a straightforward transmission of message to the receiver. The room for misunderstanding is considerable, if body is treated as a signal box: a static framework emitting and receiving strictly coded messages.... It is itself the field in which a feedback interaction takes place. It is itself available to be given as the proper tender for some of the exchanges, which constitute the social situation" (Douglas, 1975, p. 83).

There is thus, a lot of exhaustive work that has been undertaken in understanding the nuances of the body or the corporeal. Within the emerging discourse, various conditions such as AIDS or eating disorders have been given a lot of attention. Significant as they are, they pertain only to the psychological and physical difficulties resulting from a non-disabled woman placed in a different life situation. However, one category that remained/remains outside the ambit of feminism is the disabled body. Considering that disability marks the body as impaired on the basis of a biological difference and thus is a very clear reminder of the materiality of the body, the exclusion has taken some doing. The fusion of the mind and the body that takes place in the case of disabled women is indeed a site of struggle in itself. The neglect probably goes back to Descartes himself who says, "Although the whole mind seems to be united to the whole body, nevertheless, were a foot or arm or any other part amputated, I know that nothing would be taken away from my mind (Descartes, 1979, p. 97). Whether it was a result of this background or to other reasons, the reality is that the disabled body, which ideally should have been the epitome of a feminist discourse has remained at its periphery. The expectation that it should have figured is attributed to feminist tendency to accept a more subjective knowing that is inclusive of the perspectives and embodied origins of the knower. The acceptance of the mind and body dualism implicitly conveys the notion of control of one over the other.

However, what gets valorised is the control of the mind over the body and not vice versa. If it does, it is with a negative connotation. It was this neglect, which makes disability activists like Lennard J. Davis conclude that, "The disabled body is a nightmare for the fashionable discourse of theory because that discourse has been limited by the very predilection of the dominant ablist culture.The body is seen as a site of "jouissance", a native gound of pleasure, the scene of an excess that defies reason, that takes dominant culture and its rigid, power-laden vision of the body to task. The nightmare of that body is one that is deformed, maimed, mutilated, broken, diseased. Observations of chimpanzees reveal that they fly in terror from a decapitated chimp; dogs, by contrast, will just sniff at the remains of a fellow dog. That image of the screaming chimpanzee facing the mutilated corpse is the image of the critic of 'jouissance' contemplating the paraplegic, the disfigured, the mutilated, the deaf, the blind. Rather than face this ragged image, the critic turns to the fluids of sexuality, the gloss of lubrication, the glossary of the body as text, the heteroglossia of the intertext, the glossalia of the schizophrenic. But almost never to the body of the differently abled" (Davis, 1995, p. 5).

If at all feminism responded to the reality of disabled women, it was (as I mentioned in the introduction) through a 'double oppression hypothesis'. Within India, their disabilities have been neutralized too with the refrain, that being woman is the biggest form of disability. Or else the tendency is to give disability a relative position (every one is disabled in some way or another). The belief is that either oppression is common or additive. It is not difficult to see that both the realities that of disability and gender are social constructions heaped upon two biological facts: impairment and sex. Both impairment and sex become contentious, when they get situated in a social milieu that is designed to be hostile to those biological characteristics. So, if we want to understand disabled women's experiences, we need to look at how it is that sex and impairment are interpreted as negative and how they combine to form disabled women's dual oppression. Jenny Morris is absolutely right when she protests against this way of thinking which does not have any room for empowerment (Morris, 1996, p. 2).

The double oppression assumes that gender; disability, impairment, and sex are separate entities, distinguished by biological and cultural binaries. Presuming, a bio/social binary, the lives of disabled women are understood by adding the two biological foundations of sex and impairment together to conclude that disabled women are oppressed along the double axes of gender and disability. The only advantage of this approach is that, though it is initiated from biological antecedents, it does explore the constructed realities. However, such additions do not reveal the context within which the identity of the disabled woman is refuted in a context of oppression that cannot be combined or put into hierarchies. Therefore, my assertion is that issues confronting the disabled women, significant for both feminist and disability discourses, are not enough as it leaves out a critical component of disabled women's lives.

I am stating that in order for feminists and disability theorists to explore disabled women's issues, we need a radical reworking in the way we approach the body and its role in society. Notwithstanding these profound relationships with the disabled body, the neglect of the impaired body, which Lennard Davis (1995) bemoans, did not come only from those involved in the discourse of the body. The activists in the disability movement were equally reluctant to include bodies in their fight for rights. In the attempts to establish that the problems faced by disabled people do not lie in our bodies, but in the oppression that they face from the society, the disabled body got overlooked. Consequently, within the disability discourse, the apprehension was that valorisation of impairment would become self-defeating as it would fuel the individual tragedy conceptualisation, and, replicate a total disregard for society's responsibility in perpetuating disability. Considering that impaired bodies evoke revulsion and are considered deficient and abnormal, leading to a life long medicalisation, such apprehensions are not unjustified. Consequently, conflicts regarding this issue served as the bedrock for the distinction inherent in the widely accepted definition of disability that is provided by the UPIAS fundamental principles document. While this document paved the way for the recognition of disability as a social problem to be eradicated by societal change, impairment, the precursor was conceived as having close links with the medical discourse. The argument was that "disability is wholly and exclusively social", "disability [has] nothing to do with the body. It is a consequence of social oppression" (Oliver, 1996a, p. 35).

Most of these discussions as mentioned in the previous chapter were based on historical materialism, and aimed at illustrating the oppression and exclusion of disabled people. Within this context concentration on impairment was perceived as counterproductive. Tom Shakespeare, a pioneer in disability studies, has contended that, "The achievement of the disability movement has been to break our link with the bodies and our social situation and to focus on the real cause of disability i.e. discrimination and prejudice. To mention biology, to admit pain, to confront our impairments has been to risk the oppressive seizing of evidence that disability is really about physical limitations after all (Shakespeare, 1992, p. 40).

Similarly Vic Finkelstein (1996) decried the efforts of activists, who wished to attach significance to the personal experience of impairment in understanding disability. "Such work encouraged a shift away from thinking about the real world. Finding insight in the experiences of discrimination is just a return to the old file approach to expression, dressed up in social model jargon" (Finkelstein 1996, p. 11). In a similar vein, Oliver warned, that "There is a danger in emphasising the personal at the expense of the political because most of the world still thinks of disability as an individual intensely personal problem. And many of those who made a good living espousing this view would be only too glad to come out of the woodwork and say that they were right all along" (Oliver, 1996a, p. 5).

However, this position was extremely uncomfortable for many disabled men and women, but primarily women, who believed that disability is not simply a social construction, but may, at least partly reside in an objective impairment, and not just the context in which the person is situated. To the disabled feminists, the neglect of the experience of bodily change and decay reflected the masculine bias of the disability movement. Paradoxically, one of the very vocal activist who pointed out this anomaly was Paul Abberley, who articulated a need for developing a social theory of impairment as a crucial component of a social theory of disability. As early as 1987, Abberley in contrast to Oliver and Shakespeare, recognised the need to emphasise the social origin of impairment. He contended that, "By preventing disadvantage as the consequence of a naturalized impairment it legitimises the failure of welfare facilities and the distribution system in general to provide for social need, that is, it interprets the effects of social misdistribution as the consequence of individual deficiency (Abberley, 1997, p. 175).

With the intent of highlighting the social origin of impairment, he argued that while the political implications of such an analysis are apparent, the conceptual consequences also need to be analysed. Notwithstanding that such an understanding of disability, as social oppression, allows us to organise together isolated and disparate areas of social research into a lucid theoretical whole, it still results in excluding impairment from the discourse as it has been conceptualised as a medical and psychological problem to be cured or rehabilitated. Bill Hughes and Kevin Paterson (1997) have pointed out that although the impairment-disability distinction de-medicalises disability, it leaves the impaired body totally at the mercy of medical interpretation (Hughes and Paterson, 1997, p. 330). In fact, the disabled body and the meanings attached to disability have pointed out that our physical bodies are something to be embarrassed of. Further, they are to be considered as lifeless, leaking and sensory-deprived, facing a predicament in physical wellbeing and social alienation. Furthermore, the 'spectre of incontinence, leakages, smells and spillages' engenders anxiety and fear in society as a whole (Seymour, 1998, p. 19). The tragedy is that these images have been internalised to such an extent that self-perceptions of the disabled women become their own psychological monsters.

Cheryl Marie Wade cites the instance of her body giving way fully, causing both physical and psychological problems, because her activism made it difficult in accepting her limitations. She saw this emerging from images of self-sufficiency that the non-disabled likes to portray so that they do not appear as admitting weakness and vulnerability. Such images give the impression that the non-disabled is always autonomous, independent human being who needs no assistance in the process of living (Wade, 1994, p. 35). However, this tendency in a subtle manner re-enforces the personal tragedy model, as it forbids any expression of pain and vulnerability. In a way, it is like playing into the hands of the ablest hegemony, which encourages those disabled people who can best approximate the activities, and appearance of non-disabled people. These instances are of little assistance in understanding how the impaired body is constituted as the 'Other' and viewed as atypical and unfortunate. While social oppression demands the assertion that anatomy is not destiny, the body, which experiences the impairment, cannot be ignored.

These issues were pointed out early on in the disability discourse by disabled feminists such as Crow and Morris, who stressed the importance of understanding the personal experience of impairment and actualising the sentiment that "personal is indeed political". In fact, an insight into Crow's reservations regarding the social model approaches that placed impairment as biological and caused a biosocial split, is a worthwhile exercise. Bemoaning the silence of impairments from the domain of disability, Liz Crow who critiqued this silence about impairments, says, "This silence prevents us from dealing effectively with the difficult aspects of impairment. Many of us remain frustrated and disheartened by pain, fatigue, depression and chronic illness, including the way they prevent us from realizing our potentials or railing fully against disability (our experience of exclusion and discrimination). Many of us fear for our futures with progressive or additional impairments. We mourn our past activities that are no longer possible for us. We are afraid that we may die early or that suicide may seem our only option: we desperately seek some effective medical intervention: we feel ambivalent about the possibilities of our children having impairments: and we are motivated to work for the prevention of our impairments. Yet our silence about impairment has made many of these things taboo and created a whole new series of constraints on our self expression" (Crow, 1996, pp. 209-210).

Another reason for ignoring impairment has been traced to the presence of those disabled who, Wendell (2001, p. 19), labels as the 'healthy disabled'. The term is meant to refer to those people whose physical and functional limitations are relatively stable and predictable at least for a given time limit. These are people who were either born with impairments, or acquired them early in life. For stable disabilities, sickness is as uncertain as it is for the non-disabled persons. However, like I mentioned in an earlier chapter, this category may not be fixed, as stable impairments such as polio, may also change in character. As Wendell says, "illness is equated with impairment even by disability activists and scholars, in ways disability is not. Hence there is anxiety to assure non-disabled people that disability is not illness. Another consequence is the pressure to be (or to pass as) healthy disabled, both within disability activism and outside it. Disability activists have worked hard to resist medicalisation and promote the social model of disability because they feel pressured to downplay the realities of fluctuating impairment or ill health" (Wendell, 2001, p. 22).

To be acknowledged as a chronically ill disabled, people have to refrain from reminding society of their needs and limitations. Further, they have to accept a disability movement, which persists in ignoring impairment and pursues ways of improving the disabled person's economic and social conditions through materialistic means alone.

Any focus on the bodily limitations in this sense is seen as losing out in the political battle. However, what needs to be understood is that politics is not the working out of a specific stand; rather it is the insistence that the nature of the politics must remain open to question, to modification. Impairment, like abortion, cannot be governed by a simple politics. On one hand, feminists all over the world insist that it is a fundamentally political question. Yet, there would be very few in the feminist movement who would deny, that to abort is a personal choice as well. In other words, for personal choice to be a political question, the difference between private and public will have to be grasped. It is only when we engage with this question, that it is realised that what is considered as private is itself a political decision. Therefore, as Dan Goodley puts it, "Rather than viewing a turn to impairment as de-politicking, re-medicalising and watering down the social model, more and more writers are arguing that a focus on impairment, alongside an alliance with the social model and disability movement, remobilises impairment" (Goodley, 2001, p. 208).

This stance echoes with the sentiments of Hughes & Paterson, who state, "Politics today, is as much about aesthetics as it is about economic and public life". The need to re-orient the movement as well as the disability studies to incorporate impairment is imperative" (Hughes & Paterson, 1997, p. 337). Disabled feminists who have criticized the disability theory have offered resolutions, which move in the direction of altering the equations of the social model. For instance, Crow stresses that the perception of impairment as personal tragedy is merely a social construction. However, it is not the only way of thinking about impairment. An acknowledgement of the impaired body does not imply that the disabled are interpreting the experience of their bodies in a non-disabled way. Impairment, according to Crow at its most basic level, is a purely objective concept, which carries no intrinsic meaning. Says Crow, "Impairment simply means that aspects of a person's body do not function or they function with difficulty. Frequently this is taken a stage further to imply that the person's body, and ultimately, the person, is inferior. However, the first is factual information, and what follows is the interpretation. If these interpretations are socially created then they are not fixed or inevitable and it is possible to replace them with alternative interpretations based on our own experience of impairment rather than what impairments mean to non-disabled people" (Crow, 1996, p. 211).

However, doubt has been expressed regarding Crow's assumptions. To quote Alexa Schriempf, "In examining Crow's key arguments, it becomes difficult to see how her 'renewed' social model will offer a way to promote an exchange between feminism and disability, which is a key to any attempt to 'feminize' a framework" (Schriempf, 2001, p. 62). Following Schriempf, my contention is that Crow's analysis manages to reiterate the point that it is not the impairment per se, which is problematic, but it is the society's interpretation of impairment that poses problems. While an attempt to re-negotiate the meaning of impairment is there, the question about the dichotomy of impairment and disability is still not answered. The belief that they are two separate but connected things is carried forward. Crow's position is fundamentally that of being a biological foundationalist. She retains the idea that the task before the disability politics is to acknowledge the various nuances of impairment, without challenging the implication that impairment will still be understood as a 'precondition' for disability.

Thus, though, Crow's contention is to bring impairment to the forefront, I believe that, she does not problematize the biosocial split intrinsic to its biologically foundationalist thinking. In other words, a re-conceptualisation of impairment (the biological) to the realm of social is not sufficient to challenge the older understanding in which impairment is a biological given, upon which disability, the social construction, is built. Therefore, despite Crow's suggestion about re thinking impairment, the complex relations of biology and social construction are not being addressed by the disability discourse. This move does succeed in undoing the social model's inherent sexist bias in that it defends the feminist goal of politicising the personal. However, it does not provide a way for feminism and disability to be linked. It just re-enforces the belief that both disability theory and feminism cannot afford to lose sight of the body, not even for a minute. However, this insistence, which is unacceptable within the terms of patriarchal thought, does not imply any renunciation of critical thought or intellectual risk taking.

The separation of impairment from disability would resonate in the feminist minds to remind them of the classic debate about the dichotomy of sex and gender. The debates regarding the primacy of the natural body or the constructed body have been a focus of a large chunk of feminist endeavour. The assumptions have been that while there are certain natural attributes of the body that cannot be changed, the gendered cultural meanings circulating around and variously inscribing the body can be changed. Within this understanding, either sex is valorised as a biological given on which gender is imposed, or sex is negated as the conceptual enigma that obscures cultural facts about gender. Thus if women are a sex, the oppression is rooted in gender, and if women are understood as a gender, they are oppressed by sex. Both the arguments be it naturalised sex or cultural gender, result in a kind of vicious cycle. To quote Diane Elam, "The notion that there is truth to the feminine sex introduces a mode of legitimisation to feminist politics that implicitly divides and hierarchizes women between those with authoritative access to that sexual nature and those who require this instruction". She adds further that, "Hierarchy is always grounded on the assumption that differences are differences of degree, along a homogenous scale. If femininity is a natural category, then differences between women are merely the effect of degrees of false consciousness, and liberation arrives when all women have come to authoritative consciousness of their own identical, sexual identity" (Diane Elam, 1994, p. 43).

All the same there are feminists who argue that sex is not natural at all as gender is the mask, which establishes the masculine or feminine identity. In this sense, women are to be comprehended as asserting their gender identity as a common experience of oppression. Therefore the meaning of gender is understood as essentially cultural. However, this gives rise to another dilemma. Gender itself is culturally determined, in which a host of gender stipulations are there. Consequently, it is extremely difficult to determine a cause–effect relationship between gender and culture i.e. whether culture is responsible for gender stereotypes or vice-versa. There is no single position that can be thus accepted as the ultimate position.

The negation of the myth of natural sex leads to a state of disempowerment in the sense that women preserve their community by insisting that it is created by men. What actually happens is that instead of using the opportunity of examining gender differences to understand the more deeper power relations, the attempts often become instrumental in reiterating justification for these differences. As Jacqueline Rose points out, "It is not that anatomical difference is sexual difference, (the one as strictly deducible from the other) but that anatomical difference comes to figure sexual difference, that is, becomes the sole representative of what that difference is allowed to be" (Rose, 1985, p. 42).

What is evident is that despite a host of viewpoints emphatically stressing sexual multiplicity, decisions about sex and gender are made on the simplest of anatomical criteria. As Trinh Minh-ha warns, "The body is the most visible difference between men and women, the only one to offer a secure ground for those who seek the permanent, the feminine 'nature' and 'essence' remains thereby the safest basis for racist and sexist ideologies" (Trinh Minh-ha, 1989, p. 100).

The dichotomisation of impairment and disability poses a similar problem. If we were to replace impairment with sex and disability with gender, we realize that the aim of the disabled feminists is not to deconstruct gender in order to reveal the natural sex which gender has obscured. Thus, what is more important is the recognition of the complexity of both these dichotomisations within feminism and disability theory. To date, there has not been any definite way of resolving the issues posed by the dichotomy between sex and gender. This analogous situation has been pointed out by Fine and Asch in their discussion of biological foundationalism that is significant for both feminist and disability politics. They point out, "Although both movements have borrowed and profited from the black civil rights movement, these later movements share the indisputable fact that in some situations biology does and should count. However, feminism and disability rights advocates insist that instances where biology matters are extremely rare, and such cases can be minimized by changing society to better incorporate all citizens" (Fine and Asch 1988, p. 26).

It is not as if within feminism there has been no expression of discontent regarding the residue of biological determinism that is implied, and the implied isolation of gender from other categories of difference. Consequently feminists like Joan Scott have urged that a "Genuine historicization and de-construction of the terms of sexual difference needs to take place. Such a process would then shift the emphasis away from sex and onto gender so that gender could be 'redefined and restructured' in conjunction with a vision of political equality and social equality that includes not only sex but class and race" (Scott, 1988, p. 50).

Teresa de Lauretis goes a step further and proposes that the need is for a notion of gender that is not so bound up with sexual difference as to be virtually coterminous with it. According to her we need to understand this relationship in the way that gender is no longer seen either as unproblematically proceeding from biologically determined sex, or, a fantasy construct that is completely beside the point. Alternatively, she proposes that, "Gender is not a property of bodies or something originally existent in human beings rather it is a product and process of a number of social technologies which create a matrix of differences and cross any number of languages as well as cultures" (Teresa de Lauretis 1987, p. 24). A feminist conceptualisation of gender posits the subject as multiple, rather than divided or unified.

Recent theory has continued to grapple with the materialization of gendered and sexualised bodies. In her well known theory of gender, Judith Butler (1993) questions the basic presuppositions about the sex/gender relationship. Butler sees no reason to believe that sex, as natural fact, paves the way for cultural inscriptions of gender.

Therefore gender does not have the same connotation for culture as sex has for nature. In fact the discursiveness of gender element actually creates the idea of a pre-discursive sex. In this sense, sex itself is a product of gender so that gender comes before sex. In her words, "It is not that there is some kind of sex that exists in hazy biological form that is somehow expressed in the gait, the posture, the gesture: and that some sexuality then expresses both the apparent gender or the more or less magical sex. If gender is drag, and if it is an imitation that regularly produces the ideal it attempts to approximate, then gender is a performance that produces the illusion of an inverse or essence or psychic gender core.... In effect, one way that gender gets naturalized is through being constructed as an inner psychic or physical necessity"(Butler, 1991, p. 28). Thus Butler is asserting that feminists have been essentialising nature by assuming that it is devoid of history. According to her sex is already infused with meaning which is exemplified in the naming process that labels the new born as 'she' a process that is given the name of 'girling' by Butler. This process is instrumental in deciding a boundary and a repeated inculcation of a normative pattern. This girling, according to Butler, occurs through relentless restatements emerging out of a succession of exclusions, erasures, and/or marginal conditions that "not only produce the domain of intelligible bodies, but produce as well a domain of unthinkable, abject, unliveable bodies" (Butler, 1993, p. xi).

The obvious implication for an understanding of non-disabled and disabled is clearly evident, as Butler's thesis is a pointer to a critical appraisal of accepting as pure natural. To quote Nirmala Erevelles, "Butler helps to understand that impairment like sex is associated with interpellation of subjects into the semiotics of difference" (Erevelles, 2002, p. 16). It is during this process that impairment gets labelled as naturally lacking/defective and thus associated with the biological given. This results in the replications of impairment just like the girling process and thereby strengthens our understanding of the disabled body as a naturally defective category. However, this separation between the non-disabled and disabled body is maintained through performative reiterations. While these replications constitute the very bodies they manifest, they however, fail to carve an excessive realm of what Butler calls 'unintelligibility'. As Butler puts it, "The process of exclusion produces a constitutive outside to the subject, an objected outside, which is after all, 'inside' the subject as its own founding repudiation" (Butler, 1993, p. 3). In this sense the disabled bodies continue to delineate and irk the non-disabled bodies.

In commenting on Butler's work, Diane Elam says that, "We might say that gendered bodies are like actors in an unscripted play desperately trying to imitate a life that no one has led. They try so desperately because they believe that if they get it right, they would be allowed to leave the stage and lead that life" (1994, p. 50). The importance of this understanding lies in a negation of the dichotomies of sex/gender, nature/nurture and nature/culture. It is significant that Oliver the strongest advocate of the social model that dichotomises impairment and disability, himself acknowledges that experience cannot be dichotomised or simplified in his reference to 'walkers, nearly walkers, and non walkers (Oliver, 1996b, p. 100). Therefore, it becomes clear that such dichotomization, be it of sex and gender on the one hand, or, impairment and disability on the other, is problematic. It is within this context that thinkers such as Elizabeth Grosz suggest, "The body cannot be understood as a neutral screen, a biological tabula rasa on to which masculine or feminine could be indifferently projected. Instead of seeing sex as an essentialist, and, gender as a constructionist category, these thinkers [late twentieth century writers] are concerned to undermine the dichotomy" (Grosz, 1994, p. 18). Indeed, rather than speak of dichotomies at all, Grosz cites the 'Mobius strip' as a way of rethinking the relationship between body and mind. According to her, "Bodies and minds are not two distinct substances or two kinds of attributes of a single substance but somewhere in between . . .. The Mobius strip has the advantage of showing the inflection of mind into body and body into mind, the ways in which, through a kind of twisting or inversion, one side becomes another. This model also provides a way of problematizing and rethinking the relations between the inside and outside of a subject" (Grosz, 1994, p. xii).

Similarly, in realizing that dichotomization is an inaccurate representation of gender and a disability identity—as it impedes the successful bridging of feminism and disability theory—Schriempf suggests that an interactionalist paradigm should be followed (Schriempf, 2001).

While one suggestion is to get out of the binaries, the question, which arises, is about an alternative framework, which would address these issues. My contention is that one has to move away from the notion of fixity and constraint, and of the body as given towards an understanding of the body which allows for vulnerability. The need is therefore to reiterate that impairment is neither irrelevant nor a predicament. The motive in this attempt is to assert and initiate a dialogue in which there is no need to take an essentialist position of either biological foundationalism or social constructivism. This can only be accomplished if we accept that bodies are indeed a radical site for meaning and knowing. The disabled body offers a unique possibility to enable such reinterpretation. As Alexa Schriempf comments, "Because of their plasticity, their abilities to be crafted into superior beings and to break down or be injured, our bodies are at once powerful and weak, insuperable and vulnerable" (Schriempf, 2001, p. 68).

To further our understanding we need to comprehend how disability gets made. As a solution Schriempf suggests following interactionism, a term borrowed from Nancy Tuana, to understand the all-important question as to how disabled bodies get made. As the proponents of the model know, the underlying premise of interactionism is that everything is 'always already' social and material. While it might give an impression of being a radical constructivist position, it is true that material always has a considerable impact on the social. The implication of following this thought is that bodies are not pre-social nor are social systems divorced from materiality. The essential meaning of this premise is that the biological will always be entrenched in a social and cultural context. Similarly, the social can never be devoid of the biological. Thus, the boundaries between sex and gender or impairment and disability become indistinct. There can be no bio-social split in this account. "To say that the body is always already culture is not to deny that it is always already material. Rather it is to caution that a dichotomy does not have to be made out of it" (Tuana 1996, p. 60).

Tuana uses the example of bodybuilders to illustrate the fact that at the most basic level, the body is a changeable, plastic organ that challenges the unchanging boundaries between biology and culture. According to her, "Bodybuilders perform sex by transforming flesh. Culture [interacts] with biology, biology is wellspring for performativity, but it is neither fixed nor static. Nor is it a completely plastic background that the social forms into particular structures. It is active, productive, acted upon, and produced. There is a materiality that must always be taken into account, but not separated from the discursive. Indeed, the discursive is itself marked by the body (Tuana, 1996, p. 63).

Arguing that bodies are material-semiotic interactions, Tuana suggests that the complex relations between binaries should be viewed as 'emergent interplay', rather than as dichotomous (Tuana, 2001, p. 223). Within this kind of space where a move away from the binaries can be acknowledged, Tuana's proposal is that feminists make a transition from the traditional object metaphysic, wherein each object has essential and accidental characteristics with a process metaphysics that emphasizes phenomena. The latter according to Tuana views nature and nurture not as separate but as being dynamically related. Within the context of this model, Crow's argument is that impairment, at its most basic level, is an object or a fact of the body, which is interpreted by the society to mean a disability. However, to accept Crow's reasoning that impairment is objective, pre-social, and internally fixed, implies that it is impossible to challenge the deviance from an able-bodied norm implicated in the physical object metaphysic. This position however keeps the binary character of both impairment and disability intact. My submission is that impairment cannot be meaningless or factual. In fact this kind of thinking would perpetuate a biosocial split as well as create an impression that impairment itself will be always already disabling materially and culturally, as it is nothing more than deviance. The impaired body is one that never quite fits. Impairment, then can be considered a part of the social fabric like disability and not a bodily reality, owning up of which is difficult. Impairment like disability should be a signifier of not just society's response to impaired bodies, but to also illustrate how those bodies are shaped both materially and culturally. To quote Schriempf, "Labelling impairment is as value-laden and as political a practice as is labelling disability. Disability and impairment are both always about bodies in social situations and thus always about the material and social conditions of not just one's body and its abilities but also of one's environment. Classification takes place in a social context that is governed by norms that emerge, in part, out of our particular embodiments. If these norms depict certain bodies as able-bodied, then other bodies are 'always already' impaired. To have an impairment then becomes as disabling as the lack of social and physical access" (Schriempf, 2001, p. 70). As Linda Nicholson suggests, "Even to the extent that the culture itself links gender to biology, a feminist analysis that follows this approach (a feminism of difference and the biological foundationalism on which it rests) is unable to account for those who deviate" (Nicholson, 1994, p. 98). Unless feminism takes up an interactionist account, it will be of little use in aiding disabled feminists in developing a theory that can explain the gendered nature of disability or the disabling nature of gender, or include other critical locations. It will not be able to use the deviance provided by disabled women's bodies, experiences and knowledge to contribute to the growth of feminist theory. Unless that happens, the disabled body will be relegated to a sub-human terrain.

Following Foucault, Tremain argues that impairment and its materiality are naturalized effects of disciplinary knowledge/power. According to her, "Because much of work in disability studies has assumed a realist ontology, impairment has for the most part circulated in disability discourse as some objective, transcultural and transhistorical entity which biomedicine accurately represents" (Tremain, 2002, p. 34). While retaining the argument put forward by the Foucauldian approach, she further asserts that, materiality [impairment] of the body is not to be denied. Rather, "The materiality of the body cannot be dissociated from the historically contingent practices that bring it into being, that is, objectivize it" (Ibid). Following Foucault's line of argument, Tremain thus contends that impairment and its materiality are naturalised effects of disciplinary knowledge and power. She problematises the unstated premise of the social model, which dichotomises impairment and disability, thereby postulating that impairment is a necessary condition for disability. This strict division demands that, only people who have or are presumed to have impairment are counted as disabled. It is when impairment is conceptualised in this way; that the political nuances of the overcoming process are suppressed, as this analysis conceives of impairment as value-neutral. As a purely descriptive unit, the prescription inherent in it is lost. As a result, there is a failure to comprehend that this process of negotiation with the body has the potential of initiating a full-fledged war on the impaired bodies. However, the negotiation is not a straightforward exercise. In fact, the very idea of negotiation suggests that overcoming of impairment is an individualised concern. This leads to a process of legitimising of the normalising processes, which are distinctively oppressive in nature. Foucault (1988a) states that this exercise of power can be identified within processes, "which determine the conduct of individuals and submit them to certain ends" (Foucault, 1988a, p. 18). This exercise of power results in individuals adopting specific technologies of the self. These technologies are those process which Foucault says, "Permit individuals to effect by their own means or with the help of others a certain number of operations on their bodies and souls, thoughts, conduct, and way of being, so as to transform themselves in order to attain a certain state of happiness, purity, wisdom, perfection or immorality" (Ibid).

Tremain further adds that, "If we combine the foundational premise of the social model with Foucault's argument that modern relations of power produce the subject they subsequently come to represent, then it seems that subjects are produced who have impairments because their identity meets certain requirements of the medical/political system" (Tremain, 2002, p. 42). For Tremain, "If the identity of the subject of the social model—people with impairments—is actually produced in accordance with requirements of the political configuration which that model was designed to contest, then a political movement which grounds its claim to entitlement in that identity will inadvertently extend those relations of power" (Ibid).

Tremain's suggestion, to which I too would subscribe, is that what is constructed as real impairment must be identified as in the incorporated constructs of disciplinary knowledge/power that they are. A historically specific political discourse creates impairments as unitary and universal attributes of the subjects through the invocation of culturally specific norms that regulate human functioning. As Tremain adds further, "As universalised attributes of the subjects, furthermore, impairments are naturalised as an interior identity or essence on which culture acts in order to camouflage power relations that that materialised them as natural" (Ibid).

In the context of a range of meanings given to bodily beautification, modifications, fashion trends, and mutilations the significant issue is whether these constructions are ever de-constructed. It is only a thorough de-construction that can explore whether there are any subtle power struggles within which a particular struggle is embedded.

Inviting the impaired body into the discourse is to risk being labelled as essentialist or even narcissistic. My contention is that any attempt to define the external nature of social justice as separate from the body, will marginalise the profound relationships that connect the disabled bodies with who they are and how they experience oppression. To comprehend the meaning (both surface and real) of disability, the underpinning of the impaired body that precedes the disability has to be registered. The possibility of altering/changing/understanding/modifying the construction can only emerge when what the impairment signifies is understood.

As Eli Clare says, "We need to pay attention to our bodies—our stolen bodies and our reclaimed bodies. To the wisdom that tells us the causes of the injustice we face lie outside our bodies, and also to the profound relationships our bodies have to that injustice, to the ways our identities are inextricably linked to our bodies" (Clare, 2002, p. 364).

Though within the broader disability discourse, debates regarding relationship between non-disabled and disabled, impairment and disability have evoked a lot of interest and productive work, the tool for this endeavour has been identity politics. It is important to evolve an understanding of the equations involved in identity politics. Is it a boon or a bane is the ultimate question.

Identity Politics: A Bane or a Boon for the Disabled?

Disabled feminists in the west are very clearly divided on the efficacy of identity politics in taking the cause of disabled women forward. The dilemma of asserting the disabled identity remains contentious. Consequently, on one hand, there is Jenny Morris, who in her book *Pride against Prejudice*, writes about the power that collective action evokes. According to her, "The obvious challenge that we are mounting to people's assumptions was also a source of my sense of power. Indeed each time I had to explain to a non-disabled friend why I was going on such a demonstration, I was conscious of the way that this issue challenges the root of our oppression and that even to explain my motivations very briefly brings people up short against the core of their prejudice" (Morris, 1991, p. 191).

Though little more cautious, Wendell too believes that, "In separate groups of people with disabilities, powerful givens of the larger culture that put them at a disadvantage, such as non-disabled paradigm of humanity, the idealization of the body, can be challenged openly and even made irrelevant" (Wendell, 1996, p. 75). She adds further, "Although I hope that the knowledge of [the disabled] will be integrated into all culture, I suspect that any culture that stigmatises and fears disability would rather ignore and suppress that knowledge than make changes necessary to absorb it. It may have to be cultivated separately until non-disabled society is transformed enough to receive and integrate it" (Ibid).

Similarly, others like Rosemary Thomson, Carol Thomas, Helen Meekosha see the advantage of positing a disabled identity, asserting that disability provides them with a unique vantage point, which even the disabled men might not possess. The disability theory thus assumes that there is an essential disabled identity, which is set against the oppositional category of the able-bodied identity. While over the years there have been suggestions to replace the binary opposite of disabled by replacing the term able-bodied with the term non-disabled (Shakespeare and Watson, 1997, p. 293), the category of 'disability', as an identity category, has not been a matter of contest. The understanding that the disabled identity was largely unrecognised, stigmatised an invisible initiated activism to make it a subject for political recognition. The political negotiation is premised on the beliefs of activists all over the world that the need is to adopt, "A non-tragic view of disability and impairment which encompasses positive social identities, both individual and collective, for disabled people grounded in the benefits of life style and life experiences of being impaired and disabled" (Swain and French, 2000, p. 569). This realization generated a drive towards seeking public platform and forced the state to introduce legislations and other affirmative action on the lines of various other marginalized groups who have sought representation in a society that debars and discriminates against them.

This coming together of disabled community is captured very eloquently by Simi Linton, an activist in New York. Says Linton, "We are everywhere these days, wheeling and loping down the street, tapping our canes, sucking on our breathing tubes, following our guide dogs, puffing and sipping on the mouth sticks that propel our motorized chairs. We may drool, hear voices, speak in staccato syllables, and wear catheters to collect our urine, or live with a compromised immune system. We are all bound together, not by this list of our collective symptoms but by the social and political circumstances that have forged us as a group" (Linton, 1998, p. 4).

These sentiments though in different colours, have been extremely useful, as they have sought to establish an identity, which was hitherto largely neglected. As Swain and French further reify, "Disabled identity, as non-disabled identity, has meaning in relation to and constructs the identity of others. To be disabled is not to be one of those" (Swain and French, 2000, p. 577). Further, they assert that in affirming a positive identity of being impaired, disabled people are actively rejecting the dominant values of normality. "The changes for individuals are not just transforming of consciousness as to the meaning of 'disability', but an assertion of the value and validity of life as a person with impairment" (Ibid, p. 578).

These sentiments are enough proof that people labelled as deviant and deficient have actively sought the identity of being disabled by forming a collective identity that takes pride in the identity of disability. As Cheryl Marie Wade, a disabled woman poet puts it, "Many of us couldn't fit into the mainstream view of the world if we wanted to and some of us wouldn't want to if we could" (as cited in Younker, 1989, p. 31). Moreover, for most disabled people, disability describes a centrality of their lives. Says Susan Peters, "Disability flavors everything we do, whether it is the main focus of our lives or not. Whether we come to see our selves as coloured or black, crippled or disabled, these words describe an essential reality" (Peters, 2000, p. 584). In this kind of perspective, solidarity in political resistance to social oppression is used as a basis for self and social empowerment. In making personal issues into public, disabled people affirm the validity and importance of their own identity. This philosophy of asserting a marginalised identity to the exclusion of every other factor has been popularly known as identity politics.

Although the phrase 'identity politics' has been defined differently, for the present purpose I am resorting to the definition given by Gergen (1995). According to him, "[It] stands for a mode of political activism typically though not exclusively initiated by groups excluded from traditional main-stream politics. Such marginalized groups generate a self-designated identity (group consciousness) that is instantiated by the individual identities of its constituents". In this sense identity politics is different from many social movements, such as left-wing, in that the constituents of the former—such as women, Afro-Americans, gays—are politically marked as individuals. Personal, thus, is an integral part of the political. This fundamental relationship owes largely to the natural production of the political categories. One may by virtue of reason or ideology join the environment protection groups or animal saving groups. However, being a dalit, disabled or a black is not really a matter of choice. One simply is, by virtue of nature or thrown condition one of these. There is an implicit understanding that it is largely by virtue of the 'natural' condition of its members, that the groups lay claim to certain inalienable rights—for example, citizenship rights—that provide equal opportunities and rewards.

This kind of politics attaches a lot of currency/value to the formulation of a 'disabled subject'/disabled subjectivity. In fact it is deemed necessary if disabled are to achieve their political goals. The issue at hand is the modus operandi by which a collective of the disabled people will be able to fight the hegemony of the normality. The battle can be won only if the disabled act as unified subjects in their own right. Therefore, the need is to bring the disabled together, appealing to a common language, common consciousness and common experience that each disabled can identify with. It is imperative that the understanding is in terms of identity: the political subject being one who remains identical to itself in all circumstances. To be a political subject, then is to have a politically recognised identity, an identifiable self, and a consciousness to claim as one's own. Taking over from feminism this approach requires that not only would each individual woman be a subject, but also all women would partake in a common political identity called 'woman'. Extrapolating this scenario to disability politics, the politics that proceeds from this emphasis on disabled as subjects, united in a common struggle, usually going by the name 'identity politics' thus becomes a viable methodology to gain a voice which was hitherto silenced.

However, once again going by the experience of feminism, I cannot but be worried regarding the pitfalls of identity politics. To begin with it encourages uniformity and conformity. In the name of identity and consequent identification, such politics demands of the disabled that they join together solely on the basis of their commonality, so that difference among the disabled is ignored and by definition erased. The all important question that arises is, "Is it possible?" In other words, by virtue of the disabled identity functioning as a normative ideal, the disability stops being a question for disability theory. Consequently, only those who conform to the correct model of disability can hope to be a part of the political fight.

The first implication of such a belief is whether there is a collective identity of disability. However, like the subject of woman is no longer understood in terms of being a stability with a lot of disagreement as to what is it that constitutes it, or ought to constitute it, the politics of identity/difference even within the field of disability are now on the verge of confronting the developments in the last decade and a clash of multiple identities. Whether it is a contrast between the developed and the developing world, or the issues of heterogeneity and the question of multiple identities within the category of disability, (See Corker 2002; Ghai 2002a) commonality in experience of disability appears to be a deceptive category, as rarely can identity be singular in nature. Scholars such as Ayesha Vernon, have argued for a culture of political solidarity in oppression, that acknowledges multiple issues of class, severity of impairment, gender, sexuality and age. "[Each of which] can exacerbate or modify the experience of disability" (Vernon 1999, p. 394).

Within the field of disability, more than the negotiation of identity politics, the significant question for me is set against a background of multi-cultural realities in India. The question is whether it is enough to establish a hierarchy of oppressions as a response: disabled women are more oppressed than disabled men, lower caste disabled women more oppressed than high caste disabled women, the sensibility impaired (visually or hearing) are more oppressed than the mobility impaired, the developing country disabled are more impaired than the developed disabled and so on. While there would be a general agreement that all human beings lose when they are located in terms of fixed categories, it is nonetheless a gross oversimplification to say that all disabled are oppressed equally and in similar ways. However, there is another boundary problem, which is arguably more germane to the disability community since it pertains to the boundaries of disability itself. This concerns the deaf people who are classified as disabled in legislation and by society, but who repudiate the disabled identity on the grounds that they constitute a distinct linguistic and cultural minority. Another very clear illustration comes from many individuals such as the large cohort of people with cognitive and intellectual differences and mental illness, who do not get represented adequately in the disability movement. Moreover, the characteristics of disability which require attention are silenced and mainstreamed, rendering women with disabilities at a disadvantage by masking needed supports to function in the mainstream culture.

In fact this pitfall is recognised by Pratibha Parmar when she considers the ways in which identity politics employs a language of authentic subjective experience. As Parmar explains, identity politics have, "given rise to a self-righteous assertion that if one inhabits a certain identity, this gives one the legitimate and moral right to guilt – trip others into particular ways of behaving" (Parmar, 1990, p. 107). Parmar illustrates this by taking the example of women's movement, which has experienced problems because of such tendencies. Parmar adds, "There has been an emphasis on accumulating a collection of oppressed identities which in turn have given rise to a hierarchy of oppression. Such scaling has not only been destructive, but divisive and immobilizing" (Ibid).

As is clearly evident from Parmar's thesis, the danger vested in such identity politics is that both difference and identity get organised into hierarchies. The right to speak therefore, becomes a matter of collecting oppression indicators. If one can establish the authenticity of one's victimisation, one will have both moral and political rights.

While no one can deny the efficacy of collective identity in putting up a fight for social justice and equality, continuous and inevitable fragmentation of identities has made it almost impossible to develop a common vision of radical transformation. All the same how can disability politics especially with a feminist orientation speak its differences without drowning in a tide of oppression. One way in which identity politics answers this question is by analysing the voices. Who is speaking for whom? Presumably, this stance assumes that each individual should speak for the category of difference that they are seen to represent within the community. So the disabled woman is always accountable for the disability perspective and a Dalit must represent the Dalit perspective. However, this concern with visible representation and accountability can actually reflect the ways in which identity politics can exclude certain positions. So ideally an able-bodied position could dramatically change its political focus by listening to the voices of the disabled. However, this is a rather simplistic approach and can have negative consequences. For instance, the individual becomes recognizable only as representative of her/his category, which is termed as different. The disabled woman thus always represents the disabled woman's position and nothing else. That she might have any other identity is difficult to conceptualise.

Within the disability scenario, Helen Keller is a pertinent example. Whereas her popularity as a symbol of overcoming adversity is uncontested, very few people know that she was a very strong opponent of right wing policies. However she wrote with a deep sense of anguish about the responses that her political interventions evoked. Says Keller, "So long as I confine my activities to social service and the blind, they compliment me extravagantly, calling me the 'archprincess of the sightless', 'wonder woman' and 'modern miracle', but when it comes to a discussion of a burning social or political issue, especially if I happen to be, as I so often am on the unpopular side, the tone changes completely" (Keller, 1924, Cited in Crow, 2000, p. 854).

While the vulnerability of disability is accorded an inflated status, another disadvantage is that one individual is assumed to be able to represent an entire identity category. That, there could be differences between the visually impaired or women is not easily recognised. Thus, the lesbian woman or the physically disabled woman is supposed to represent all lesbian women and all physically disabled women under the implicit assumption that all of them share the same opinions. The result of this form of identity politics is that in ensuring representation, it can actually lead to tokenism and stereotyping. There may also be some merit in remembering Young (1990) warning that communities are often conjured out of the yearning to be among similar-and-symmetrical selves, to the point where members respond to alterity by overthrowing it beyond their border. In this sense a self perpetuating spiral is set into motion, whereby the tighter the boundaries are drawn, the more those included will normalise their sameness and exclude others. The more the excluded will become estranged others, the less the community will be informed by experiences of and reflection upon diversity. However, going by the experience even of the disability movement in India, any movement which finds its voice oppressed within the culture more generally, will soon find that within its own ranks some voices are more equal than others. In the thrust toward economic equality, women turn on men for their patriarchal disposition; in the drive toward gender equality, elite middle class are found guilty of silencing the lower non-elite voice, the educationally privileged guilty of exclusionary language, the straight for politics detrimental to the lesbian, and so on. However, this should not undermine the fact that a political movement has to identify who it is fighting for, what its values are, and how it wants to bring about change.

Thus, diverse cultural groups with similar political agendas not only remain separated, but frequently compete with one another to achieve the same outcome i.e. equal opportunity. Thus even if one acquires the capacity to name oneself as special, such as disabled, it cannot guarantee on its own the material conditions and resources necessary for social thriving, as identity is always produced through interaction shaped in part by other's definitions.

Given these realities, a significant question to my mind is regarding the fate of those who are marked with "multiple categories of difference". Is a dalit disabled poor woman, first a dalit, then poor, and then a disabled woman? With whom should she seek a poltical alliance that would profit her the most? This is where identity which is understood in terms of fixed nuances creates the greatest trouble. Perhaps at this stage it would be wise to recall some instances from the history of feminism. What is striking in this is the position of prominent black intellectual women. Patricia Hill Collins has written about the necessity for a specifically black feminist movement. However, she also advocates a critical stance towards mainstream, feminist, and Black scholarly inquiry (1997). Here she joins other prominent black thinkers, along with a cadre of Native American and Asian-American women in challenging feminism for its implicit racism and its overarching concern with white, middle-class women's issues.

While I realise that in my own location in India, where disability issues are highly marginalized and invisible, nothing short of a collective action on the part of the disabled can lead to their empowerment. So in one sense it does seem ironical that just at the point when disability issues are gaining a recognition in the public arena and the disabled are reaching a position where they are feeling able to write themselves as subjects, I am contesting the idea of a stable disabled identity. I am in fact reminded of a rather pertinent question asked by Nancy Harstock in the context of feminism. Says Harstock, "Why is it that just at the moment when so many of us who have been silenced begin to demand the right to name ourselves, to act as subjects rather than objects of history that just then the concept of subjecthood becomes problematic" (Harstock, 1990, p. 163). Similarly, responding to a critique of identity politics, bell hooks says, "Yeah it is easy to give up identity, when you have got one" (hooks, 1990, p. 163). However, I also understand that merely stressing the issues of identity is not enough. Being a disabled does not imply that you are instinctively an activist. A constant struggle with the self is needed in order to reject the 'normality' definitions. Therefore, it is important to retain a self critical component within the larger struggle of asserting the rights and identity.

Notwithstanding the fact that identity politics is a contested terrain, it is worthwhile to recall the political character of both. The disability movement has often been understood as most powerful when it grounds itself in essentialist notions of disability. The question however is whether the notion of difference can break out of the vicious cycle in which disabled are self evident. In other words, is it possible to have a disability politics, which does not have to rest on a notion of disabled identity, or on an essence, which would seek its political realisation? How can we as feminists disabled or otherwise acknowledge differences, without resorting to a vortex of the hierarchy of oppression?

Possibly, it is worthwhile to register the fact that the rhetoric of rights operates as a mechanism of both inclusion and exclusion. For those who are in a position to take care of their own interests and or /have adequate assistance to apply for services of one's choice and if necessary appeal, legislations can be of great value indeed and a means for greater inclusion. As Ruth Lister has so aptly formulated, "Autonomy and agency that derives from rights can only be made possible by the human relationships that nourish them and the social infrastructure that supports it" (Lister, 1997, p. 114). In this sense the identity of the disabled presumes a certain stability of mostly tangible impairments as evidence of a bona fide disability identity, which clearly marginalises those with non-apparent impairments such as learning disability. Whilst the reluctance or refusal to differentiate between impairments by identifying them, augments the claims of people with apparent impairments that they represent all disabled people. The problems come when there are people who are coming to see themselves as disabled in spite of not being recognised as disabled in traditional discourses. For example, can a dark or fat woman be called disabled? The additional hurdles are encountered when those whose disabilities have been invisible even apparently question the hierarchy of impairments. As is the case right now the people with learning disabilities, as well as autistic have been left out of the Indian legislation. Regarding disabilities there may be again a marginalisation as they experience other hierarchies of orthodoxies and oppressions. Similarly, within the Indian cultural scenario, mental illness is as stigmatising as any physical illness.

Within the disability politics, the issues of identity have retained a binary character. Therefore, it has not interrogated the drawbacks of postulating an essential identity of the disabled woman. Moreover, it has not questioned whether this identity is going to be contingent on the stability of unified body image. And, if one counts a disabled woman only for political reasons, isn't disability becoming just another identity category? Taken in this form it is difficult to imagine how it might seem to disturb other categories or the boundaries that seem to separate us from one another. Consequently, if identity is only reinforcing/ reiterating distinctions by playing into the same hierarchical system, can there be a way out?

However, if this identity is serving its purpose, then there is merit in keeping it alive and vibrant. As Price and Shildrick maintain, "Both personal identity—the sense of a unified unchanging and bounded self, a base perhaps from which to demonstrate autonomous agency—and group identity—with its emphasis on knowing who is to count as the same, seem to manifest a nostalgia for the modernist values of separation and exclusion. Perhaps all politicised groupings face the question of counter identity, which promises the power of solidarity in challenging group devaluation, whilst at the same time demanding the policing of its own boundaries and the marginalisation of difference just as surely as does unmarked identity" (Price and Shildrick, 1998, p. 235).

Thus it is important to be a little wary of accepting such practices. While it is true that they interrogate norms and labels, leading to an identification of the problems inherent in them, we need to be cautious.

As, Spivak warns, to be critical of stand point epistemologies that presume that a person's identity assures a definite experience or knowledge of the world, reminding us that class consciousness and class position do not necessarily coincide (Spivak, 1988, pp. 277-278). It would be wise to remember that to represent the other is to confront or indulge in our own narcissism because "people are different from the object of emancipatory benevolence" (Spivak, 1990, p. 136).

In voicing my doubts, I am not denying that significant gains have accrued by resorting to identity politics. Whether it was in the form of visibility or legislation or an inclusion into the national census. It was through a collective process of writing oneself as subjects that these dreams became realities. Identity, however, is neither natural nor stable and the problem of identity politics is to assure that it is. The kinds of tensions, which are evident in Corker's work, clearly demonstrate that we definitely need to pay attention to hierarchical structure of difference that focuses on an acceptance of fixed boundaries. As Julia Epstein puts it, "The normal, even when understood to represent a curve or continuum remains an inchoate conception of a lack of difference, of conformity, of the capacity to blend in invisibly" (Epstein, 1995, p. 11). Under the regime of normality every one must fear becoming a member of the group designated as the Other. It might be worthwhile to recall that aging points out to the material vulnerability of the healthy body. Such a recognition has the potential to assert that the difference between one body and the other in terms of a normative ideal might not remain sustainable over time. While it might explain the underlying anxiety and the experiential terrain of disease that disability invokes, it is also suggestive to use Price and Shildrick's term, "of the ethical fatuity of the process of Othering" (Price and Shildrick 1998, p. 236).

A more thoughtful politics of disability, therefore, would attempt to disrupt the norms of dis/abled identity by divulging the failure of those norms to ever fully and finally contain a definitive standard. It would be more accurate to understand identity as a production "which is never complete, always in process and always constituted within, not outside representation" (Stuart Hall, 1994, p. 76). A recognition of common political goals can definitely assist the building up of a social movement. However, the fact that the movement can be splintered by ignoring the internal differences has to be recognised. While we are doing this, we cannot ignore the crucial questions of how will we decide to put aside our differences? How will a position of political solidarity be arrived at?

I would like to take recourse to an important corrective offered by Trinh Minh-ha. She argues that, "Difference understood not as an irreducible quality but as a drifting apart within 'woman' articulates upon the infinity of 'woman' as entities of inseperable 'I's' and Not – 'I's' . . .. (Trinh Minh-ha, 1989, p. 104). Difference does not annul identity. It is beyond and alongside identity . . .. The idea of two illusory separated identities, one ethnic, the other woman (or more precisely female), again partakes in the Euro American system of dualistic reasoning and its age old divide—and conquer tactics". Trinh's challenge is a reminder of the problems that disabled women have had with dichotomisation of impairment and disability.

My submission both as a psychologist and a disabled woman is that, identity has to be understood as a constant movement. As Chantal Mouffe (1992) puts it, "Identity is best described as an ensemble of subject positions that can never be totally fixed in a closed system of differences, constructed by a diversity of discourses among which there is no necessary relation, but a constant movement of overdetermination and displacement" (Mouffe, 1992, p. 372). I think the all important query is not what ontological status implies or means. Rather, what is its significance?—patronisation or pride, deviance or difference and the webs of significance that are spun through human agency about these conditions. In other words, we should ask, What is the importance assigned to disability? By whom? Finally, can this understanding of difference count enough to make a political difference? Judith Butler makes a similar point when she urges us to be critically queer. To quote Butler, "And if identity is a necessary error, then the assertion of queer will be necessary as a term of affiliation, but it will not fully describe those it purports to represent. As a result, it will be necessary to affirm the contingency of the term: to let it be vanquished by those who are excluded by the term but who justifiably expect representation by it, to let it take on meanings that cannot now be anticipated" (Butler, 1993, p. 230). She further points out the fact that, "The feminist 'we' is always and only a phantasmatic construction, one that has its purposes, but which denies the internal complexity and indeterminacy of the term and constitutes itself only through the exclusion of some part of the constituency that it simultaneously seeks to represent" (Ibid).

However, the fragile status of the 'we' should not worry us. The only issue at stake is that while any identity is being asserted politically, the fluidity of that identity category must be thoroughly analysed and recognised. To end, it seems pertinent to point that a celebration of differences can be paradoxical. In some ways assertion of specific categories based on differences reinforces the divisions existing in the given social order, leaving them unshaken. Moreover, an enthusiastic embracing of all the categories succeeds only in categorising and not in finding resolutions. One is reminded of Audre Lorde who writes, "As a forty nine year old Black feminist socialist mother of two, including one boy, and a member of an interracial couple, I usually find myself a part of some group defined as Other, deviant, inferior, or just plain wrong" (Lorde, 1981, p. 114). Though location is definitely helpful in delineating such facts of history, it leaves the problem of identity without any cross-examination. As Christina Crosby cautions, "Consciously assuming a specific stand point is to assume that ontology is the ground of epistemology, that who I am determines what and how I know. But how do I know who I am? That's obvious: I am my differences which have been given to me by history. In this circle, the differences which seem to refract and undo a substantive identity actually reflect a multifaceted, modified but all too recognisable subject" (Crosby, 1992, p. 137).

While as a disability activist in the Indian scenario, I definitely wish to challenge the biological determinism inherent both in disability and gender, I am exhausted by the celebration of the idea that there are essential differences between disabled and non-disabled or disabled women and non-disabled women. It is true that efforts need to be made to include the marginalised categories such as disabled women who are effectively speechless, and excluded, perhaps it is better to leave these ideas in tension to resist any kind of foreclosure which could both academically and politically be unwarranted. Certainly feminism needs to become sensitive to the issues of difference. As

Hannah Arendt put it so aptly, "Everybody sees and hears from a different position. This is the meaning of public life . . . . Only where things can be seen by many in a variety of aspects without changing their identity, so that those who are gathered around them know they see sameness in diversity, can worldly reality truly and reliably appear . . . . The end of the common world has come when it is seen only under one aspect and is permitted to present itself in one perspective" (Arendt, 1958 , pp. 57-58).

Thus, the issue is not of deciding which is the most oppressive reality or the worst evil. Rather, this fragmentation is itself a part of the problem. It mirrors the linear social order made up largely of patriarchal thoughts, overlooking the deep complexities of human existence. It is absolutely essential that one understands that any identity is composed of different components out of which, political, cultural and individual are extremely significant. What is needed is a process in which, development takes place to over-ride a pessimistic self-image with impairment, with a positive self image with disability as social exclusion. While a collective awakening is definitely an asset, it can be accomplished through a personal growth. I strongly believe that both the collective and personal have to be conjoined together to bring about a change in the quality of life of those labelled as disabled.

5

Moving Towards a More Inclusive Feminism: Re-thinking Disability

> *Struggles for a different allocation of resources and resistance to categorization are one and the same thing . . . . Whether or not there is an explicit call to arms in these terms, something that can be called self-assertion — or 'human spirit' is at the core of resistance to domination . . . . It is as intrinsic, and as necessary, to that social life as the socializing tyranny of categorization.*
>
> Jenkins (1996, p. 175)

As has been clear from the previous chapters, being born less-than-perfect in a society, which valorises perfection, is akin to having committed a capital offence. The felony assumes grave intensity when those who are labelled imperfect are contending with indifference and oppression within a women's movement in which the able body norm is seldom questioned. The neglect though bemoaned has rarely been a serious concern. However, the issue cannot be resolved by just admitting to a complete exclusion of the concerns of disabled women. The impasse can be as stifling as the exclusion. What one needs therefore, is an articulation of ideas that have the potentiality of changing the scenario. My intention in the preceding chapters was to highlight the complexities of the lives of disabled women. The first objective has been to share with the feminists, the meaning of being disabled. While I have drawn upon my own and my fellow disabled women's experiences, I have shared my unhappiness with attempts that position disability as the sole pre-occupation of those who are given that label. It is true that much of what I have shared has stemmed from the epistemic contingency of the disabled. The reality as it stands today is that very few non-disabled feminists have chosen to understand disability, However, I do not believe that a non-disabled woman cannot traverse the same road that a disabled can. In my own understanding, disabled women too like the non-disabled women, can occupy multiple positions that are taken as responses to the kind of domination that is experienced most critically.

My endeavour therefore has been to present before the readers 'bodies' that get dis (embodied) because of constructions that create a total invisibility of the disabled woman. Mostly constructions of disability assume that the disabled person is more damaged while those who construct this disabled identity are undamaged. The implicit assumption of course is that society is normal, intact, capable of setting norms. However, no one questions the authenticity of this rather utopian expectation of a perfect/undamaged society. The work of reconstructing the society often focuses on the material conditions of oppression. It is for this reason that it is significant to understand that disabled women embody a complex of interlocking situations. To quote Eli Clare, "Gender reaches into disability; disability wraps around class; class strains against abuse; abuse snarls into sexuality; sexuality folds on top of race . . . . Everything finally piling into a single human body" (Clare, 1999, p. 123).

While, it is true that there are sensitive women, who have heard the voices of their disabled relatives, colleagues and friends, however within the broader feminist discourse and practice, a certain tokenism prevails. While no one would refute the importance of understanding disability, actual and concrete efforts are seldom made. That, this resistance comes from those who are raising their voices against oppression, can be a painful reality. The scenario thus has the potentiality of creating a deadlock, which in any event is not of much assistance if the issue of disability has to move forward.

It is with this thought that I endeavour to think aloud regarding the inter-relationship between the feminist discourse and practice and the lives of those who live with the stigma of disability, as inclusion from the vantage point of a disability activist, is the only hope. Yet I am fully aware of the fact that hope at times is an extremely accomplished liar. When I say this I am 'hoping' to communicate to my readers the complications of evolving an inclusive discourse. Nevertheless, my firm belief is that (even though in present times, it might appear utopian to some and to some a grandeur delusion of a schizophrenic), a just society can evolve only if all the members of the community they inhabit accept each other. This process does not call for a negation of differences, but understands that it is a social judgement that defines a particular difference as 'difference' that counts.

The question thus is not whether we perceive differences, but rather what meaning is brought to bear on those perceived differences. Rather than viewing a difference simply as an intrinsic deficiency, as is the case of impairments and disabilities, one can comprehend it as a matter of context. This can open possibilities where for instance, physical arrangements can be altered to create a situation in which difference does not emerge as another term for liability. To understand fully its impact, however, not only calls for a concerted effort, but also a certain degree of empathy and sensitivity. Living in the body that is marked by impairment, cannot be appreciated till one leaves oneself open to experiencing its realities. As Nancy Mairs a fellow disabled recounts "...Not long ago a friend called me intrepid. But I'm only as brave as I have to be, I reminded her. And I don't want to have to be this brave (Mairs, 1996, p. 48). Thus disability is not only a question of social exclusion, it is very much concerned with experiences of the impaired body.

However, communication of such messages create a certain amount of anxiety as the instability of the disabled body is also an indicator of one's own instability. During my growing years (and it happens now also) I remember falling down on innumerable occasions. The physical hurt, though tough at times, was always less than the looks of fear on the faces of those around me. As Janet Price and Margrit Shildrick (2002) say, "The dis-integrity and permeability of bodies, the fluctuations and reversibility of touch, the inconsistency of spatial and morphological awareness, the uncertainty of future, are all futures that may be experienced with particular force in the disabled body, but they are by no means unique to it"(Price and Shildrick 2002, p. 74).

However, the other disabled person is an acute reminder of these unconscious as well as conscious fears. It is only when it is understood that both impairment and disabilities are social constructions that acknowledging difference becomes easy. For this increases the possibility that would make the non-disabled women interrogate the label of disability. How many of us, for example, would label another person disabled, if we have to face them and look squarely in the eye and say, "You are out of the reckoning, because of the kind of the choices we made. We constructed an inaccessible world in which you do not fit: therefore the only choice is to stay out as a special category". My hunch is that the number is not going to be very large. Thus, what is urgently required is the necessity of collaboration between the non-disabled world and the disabled world to engage with each other. The imperative need is to acknowledge that both disability studies and feminism are struggling with some critical questions, for which there are no readymade answers, as there are very few aspects of lives that tie women together naturally. To quote Haraway, "There is nothing about being a female that naturally binds women. There is not even such a state as being female, itself a highly complex category constituted in contested sexual scientific discourses and other social practices. Gender, race or class consciousness is an achievement forced on us by the terrible historical experience of the contradictory social realities of patriarchy, colonialism and capitalism" (Haraway, 1989, p. 179).

Notwithstanding this reality it is difficult to negate that differences have stemmed into a kind of vicious cycle, where sometimes they work only as slogans which are self evident. The effect is that they create dichotomies; you either are for the cause of disabled women or you are not. As Jean Baudrillard comments, "In academy we are confronted with a duopoly, a structure of simultaneous oppression which seems agonistic but is relatively stable" (Baudrillard, 1983, p. 134). What then gets overlooked is the possibility of treating differences in a innovative way. It is only when this is accomplished that we will be able to contribute to a process which would fulfil what Haraway calls the feminist scholar's need for "an earth-wide network of connections, including the ability to translate knowledge among very different—and power-differentiated—communities" (Haraway, 1991, p. 187). She adds further, "we need the power of modern critical theories of how meanings and bodies get made, not in order to deny meaning and bodies, but in order to live in meanings and bodies that have a chance for the future" (Ibid).

One instance of how difficult and taxing, this endeavour can be is evident from Dibernard's work. As a non-disabled university professor, she undertook an introductory course in disabled women's poetry. Her sense of ease with teaching was, in her words, "quickly shattered the first night when a woman in the wheel chair wheeled into the room" (Dibernard, 1996, p. 132). "I knew then", says Dibernard, "that I have lot of work to do in coming to terms with my own relationship with and feelings about disability and my identity as an able bodied person" (Ibid). In confronting disability, Dibernard not only faces the epistemic challenge of coming to grips with the reality of disability, she reconceives of her identity as located within able-bodiedness, "I feel now my identity not as a woman who happens to be able bodied, but as a woman whose able-bodiedness is a location for which I need to take responsibility" (Ibid). In acknowledging able bodiedness as a site from where she experiences the world, she retrieves her embodiment. However, for this negotiation to take place her encounter with disability was a must. Though a detailed account is not within the scope of the present chapter, Dibernard's newly found location only enables her to perceive herself not as someone who happens to be able bodied, but as someone who *is* able bodied. Yet, whether this can transform the conceptualisation of disability remains a significant question.

This explains the reason for the disabled women's experience of negation. Whether it is wheelchair/crutches/cane or any other disability marker, the non-disabled people, both men and women, ignore the person who is using them. As symbolic interactionism tells us, we are always searching for symbols as a base for expressing ourselves to others and for self-identity. Symbols like a wheelchair or a white cane, creates/determines social meaning rendering the perception of disabled as dependent and different. The difficulties, however, do not end there, as, while the perception of others has a definite impact, there is also a reciprocal reaction to that perception. This reaction further influences those who perceive and in turn influences the concerned person. Thus, Mead (1995) argues that an individual may lose a body part, and yet not be affected in their conception of self. However, the public scrutiny and devaluation discredits the individual as a fully functioning person. As is evident, many disabled women have to counteract the belief of others that they have met with a tragic fate that warrants pity.

Like a fellow disabled Sarla, a polio survivor, shares her experience.

"There are times, when other people's conception of my tragedy gets to me. I have to endlessly hear that it is amazing that I work and

I am married! And my husband does not have a disability. It ends up giving the message that I should consider myself special and lucky just because a non-disabled has chosen to spend his life with me and we are a happy family" (Personal Communication).

Such reactions have to be understood in terms of the overcoming hypothesis that has been discussed in the context of medical model outlined in the first chapter. When disabled people are seen in roles that are not advocated for them, it lessens the fear that disability carries for the non-disabled. Interestingly the implicit assurance in such instances is that being normal is right and should be the ultimate goal. The expectation, therefore, is to fight back. If you succeed, the reward will be admiration and praise. This might even appear as preferable to the construction, which looks at the disabled as an object of pity or writes them off as invalid. However, while this might achieve the status of a performing artist, it does not imply admission to the circles of normality.

For full inclusion, each woman within a culture needs to see herself as an unfinished story, coming to terms with the stories of others and making an attempt to explore the ways in which these stories intertwine. If this happens, assumption of an abyss of difference won't be needed. Instead the merging of stories would be a good reason for people to, "Represent...themselves to each other and to themselves as unfinished autobiographies or narratives. In formulating these autobiographies people define themselves in terms of commitments to... projects, ranging from short-term projects... to the projects through which they define the significance of their lives" (Gare, 1996, p. 360).

It is only with this process of negotiation, that one can comprehend that understanding disabled women in a social vacuum is not possible. The culture within which they are embedded also needs to be given attention.

One aspect of this understanding lies in the realisation that while disabled women experience oppression in many forms for which their feminist sisters are definitely not responsible, there are certain disciplinary practices of physical normalcy which need to be questioned by the feminists more thoroughly than has been done before. It does not take very long for the disabled women to absorb and internalise that though all of us have been given bodies, not all bodies are considered equal. Some appear beautiful, some average and some are, quite frankly, discardable. My own understanding is that this applies to any woman who deviates from the normative standard, and who, to borrow Wendell's terminology, is caught in a 'window dressing' of normalcy. It is quite difficult to detach from the messages that get communicated from the society. These messages say something as fundamental as the fact, that we are not likely to see a Ms. Universe or Ms. World with a pair of crutches. They expect you to be of a certain height, weight, and 'beautiful' (whatever that means). The predominance of the beauty myth has made aesthetic stratification as powerful as class, caste, gender stratification (Synnott, 1993, p. 101), and aesthetic relationships have become a significant factor in the oppression of disabled people (Hughes, 1999).

As Synnott (1993) states, "Beautyism, and its attendant fascism, the prejudice and discrimination in favour of the beautiful and attractive (however defined) and against the ugly and less attractive are virtually institutionalised in our society and are the last major bastion of inequity . . .. The pursuit of beauty... is widely regarded as an excellent investment with substantial psychic, social and economic returns and for those reasons it is increasing in salience... [all] around the world" (Synnott, 1993, p. 100). The body thus has become a project, that is agreeable to cosmetic surgery, diet control, preventive measures for aging, creating the impression that we are in a position to choose and shape our bodies. When such aesthetic ideals of embodiment are advocated, the obvious implication is that an impaired body signifies failure. Contending with less than subtle messages that their bodies won't ever measure in an environment where even a dark skin is enough to feel endangered, disabled women are bound to live with a concurrent sense of oppression that has both external and internal determinants.

Another area of concern for a full inclusion of disabled women into the feminist world is to initiate the participation of disabled women together in national conferences and meetings, where issues such as reproductive rights, sexuality and self-advocacy are issues of concern and debate. In a country like India, this is not as simple as it might appear. For to strike an alliance with the disabled women, the women's groups have to first evaluate the built environment. This participation is significant. Many feminists who are concerned about the neglect of the disabled women's issues from the Indian discourse, feel that one reason for neglect is a lack of existential statements from the disabled women. As they don't get shared at public platforms, they do not get internalised by the women's movement. This highlights the scant attention that is paid to, what is termed in the disability vocabulary as, the issue of access. I have to struggle hard to recall Indian seminars or conferences, where this concern of the disabled women has been addressed. Notwithstanding the kind of impairment, access is significant for all of them. For those who love walking and consider climbing three flights of stairs a pleasure, the difficulties that a mobility impaired woman might experience is often not realised. Similarly, the unavailability of the text or the stress on the spoken word marginalises the visually and hearing impaired women. The organising authorities are thus unaware that the way in which the conferences/seminars/meetings are patterned, does not give the impression that they are sensitive to human subjectivity of those who bear the mark of being bodily different. In a way the design apartheid coupled with the lack of accessible information reinforces the non-disabled/able-bodied values. As Davies and Lifchez comment "how one feels about a place, how one interprets it, or even whether one can adequately interpret it—these all are less quantifiable, but important, aspects of accessibility. A place...that causes [people] a minimum of pain, frustration, and embarrassment is more accessible than a place that confuses, harasses, or intimidates people" (Davies and Lifchez, 1987, p. 40).

A focus on the arrangements which recognise the intricate relationship between spatiality and the quality of disabled women's lives can only come from feminists, who are vigilant of such inscriptions. More than a feminist response, this would also be an ethical response. Only when disabled women are given the conditions which are not only their right, but which minimise disadvantage, can the existential concerns get shared with a feminist audience. My work here is thus, an attempt to forge an alignment with the feminist community, so that a change in public policy can be mediated. One hopes that next time there is a conference on public policy under the auspices of women's studies, there will be an inclusion of disabled women and their needs. It is true that not all bodily limitations can be compensated by spatial arrangements and innovative technology. Yet it is only in the space between such limitations, that there remain many unexplored avenues for comfortably accommodating a wide range of mind-bodies. Moreover, a deconstruction and (re)construction of space/technology might benefit many other bodies who are not traditionally impaired. While universal sisterhood might not be as acceptable as it was, the reality is that though dealing with difference might have broken up the singular stand point theory, it has only changed the question of 'who am I?' in the strict Eriksonian sense, to 'who are we?' The categorical shift, however, is important as it has the potential of becoming more inclusive.

It is difficult to leave the vision of a feminist rendering of disability, if one excludes the concern of care giving and care receiving. In recent years some debates have taken place (See Davar 1999) that have weighed the paradigms of care in terms of the ethics of care versus the ethics of justice. Davar in her discussion warns that, "Care must be problematised first, for its psycho-politics" (Davar, 1999, p. 208). This implies that feminists need to assess 'who' benefits from this and, 'what' are the circumstances and consequences for the women who practice care. However, when Davar issues this cautionary note, she is unfortunately not thinking of a large number of disabled women who are in constant need of care. Moreover, even their mothers who are major stakeholders languish in isolation both in feminist theory and practice. That there is often an underestimation of the needs of disabled people in feminist writing is exemplified in Davar's work on women as carers which highlights the burden women carry as a consequence of being in familial networks. The emphasis is on the the ones who care. It personifies Hilary Graham's statement that, "Caring is a shorthand way of talking about what carers feel and do rather than what care receivers feel and do" (Graham, 1993, p. 463). Feminists have always insisted upon autonomy and independence as the guiding principles of any feminist endeavour. While recognising the embeddedness of women's lives in networks of family and society, insistence has been on one's own freedom. Perhaps that is the reason which creates the desire for physical fitness and competence. However, disabled women are in no position to aspire for this freedom. Therefore, the concept of equality, which demands that people should be treated equally falls short when it comes to disabled women who need care.

Having an impairment means being in a vulnerable position because of dependency. This dependent relationship has been known to lead to a pattern in which there is a suspension of basic rights related to respect, privacy and personal choices (Young 1990). Power is unequally distributed within these kinds of relationships. Requiring the help and support of others in order to pursue everyday activities such as dressing and undressing, eating, moving, or, pursuits of an intellectual nature in adult life, means that power remains with those who provide support. I wish to submit that no one and that definitely includes non-disabled women, is entirely self sufficient and the construction of disabled women as exclusively recipients of care is not true. Instead of constructing the disabled women as special and burdensome dependents, I argue that we in India, have always been an interdependent society. However, this does not imply that I do not recognise the problems inherent in this interdependence. I agree fully with Morris's (2001) warning against the recognition of carers as a 'sole oppressed group'. It increases the oppression of individual disabled people and strengthens the negativity associated with disability. A feminist political analysis of care giving that takes as its vantage point only the caregiver's pressures, ignores the cared, who are constructed as passive, dependent and in a recipient role. While Morris in her own context is worried about the implications of political analysis from the perspective of the care receiver, in India, both the giver and the receiver have been dreadfully ignored by the feminist analysis.

Consequently, neither have the feminists affirmed the institutionalised patterns of care, which are largely non-existent, nor have they conducted any analysis of the unequal power relationship between the parents and the disabled children/adults. Needless to add, the major stakeholder in the process of caring is the mother. The amnesia regarding both the mother and her disabled daughter is thus complete. In this context Davar's call for analysing the labour dimension, as being central to women who are by and large socialised into being good carers within the Indian milieu is important. Says Davar, "What is problematic in these situations is not that women have been human enough to care, but that they have to take on an overload of caring functions within the household leaving them mentally exhausted" (Davar, 1999, p. 229). The twin studies of Arora and Ghai (1997) and Mangla and Ghai (2000) have indicated the trauma that the mothers of disabled daughters face. Valuable as these works are, they all fail to think about 'caring' from the perspective of the one who is a recipient. Morris's caution is thus a pointer to the feminist analysis which can fill up a lacuna if it were to undertake research that explores caring from the perspective of both the disabled and their caretakers.

Barbara Hillyer (1993) who writes from the location of both, being a mother, with a developmentally disabled daughter, and a feminist, shares her experience of excessive demands on her as a mother. She also conceptualises the relationship with her daughter, within a scenario, where there is a constant interaction with professionals from all walks of life. She finds that these interactions discount the knowledge regarding her daughter, subjecting her to greater institutionalised control, bureaucratic monitoring and social judgements regarding the quality of care. Her experience is that society exploits a mother's care giving, often making her a scapegoat for anything that happens to the child. Such a reaction would probably resonate in the mothers who have disabled children, especially daughters in India, where there are additional problems because of a lack of a fully functioning support system. Davar, Morris and Hillyer though in different contexts indicate the necessity of understanding the political context of care giving from the vantage point of a woman. Who can be better equipped than feminists to understand these political nuances and offer correctives?

Another area of concern is the possibility of disabled women often experiencing subtle abuse being controlled, rather than in control of caring relationships. Most of the women who shared their experiences with me (See chapter two) feared abuse and violence more from the extended family and acquaintances. In this sense though the family is not directly responsible, it does lead to a 'fear psychosis' as many of their accounts are treated as overactive imagination. As Neelima expressed her disgust, "I tried telling my mother about my uncle". She had such a look of disbelief as she said the following to me, *"Arre woh tumhe kyno tang karega. Usko ladki ki kami hai? Tumne kabhi apne aap ko shishe mein dekha hai?* (Why would he be interested in you? Is he short of girls outside? Have you ever seen yourself in the mirror?)" (Personal Communication). The work on sexual abuse albeit with 'normal' women resonates with this kind of 'disbelief' reaction from the parents. As Hendy and Pascal comment, "The risk of assault and rape from acquaintances is generally greater than that from strangers. Women with disabilities are especially vulnerable; being less able to defend themselves...the nature of caring relationships and violence within caring relationships are less well-advertised issues than are risks from strangers or intimate partners . . . ." (Hendy and Pascal, 1998, p. 418). What does get advertised though again, not very often is the strain that carers experience. Without undermining the value of their support, it has to be acknowledged that what gets ignored is the undermining of the person being cared for. As Oliver and Bob Sapey state, "The recognition of care givers is itself part of the problem because it reinforces the helper-helped relationship that lies at the heart of the creation of dependency, by seeing the needs as relative to the 'burden' caused by the disabled person . . . .. The demand therefore for more support on the carer needs is to both ignore the reality of the situation and to attribute blame to the disabled person" (Oliver and Sapey, 1999, pp. 105-107).

Finally, at this juncture what is probably significant to understand is the politics of control, which gets activated through the nature of the 'gaze'. Gaze has been historically established, pervasive, powerful, gendered and engendering structure of control and dominance in a given culture. As feminists argue, the gaze is male. It conveys appropriation, leading to an objectification of woman. It is never simply an act of vision, nor can it ever be seen as neutral or non-judgemental. As a regulative and asymmetrical system of control, the gaze is fundamental factor in what Teresa de Lauretis (1987) has termed the 'technologies of gender'.

My contention is that in case of the disabled women, it is not only the male gaze, but also an able bodied gaze, which has to be encountered. Michel Foucault in this regard has provided one of the most influential theories presenting a illuminating discussion of the close links between the subject/object relations in structures of looking. In his discussion of Bentham's 'panopticon' in his book, *Discipline and Punish* (1977) in particular, Foucault describes the relations between power, visibility and vulnerability, and between control and subjection. The panopticon is an architectural structure, a building designed upon the principles of an optical system of control and discipline. Open, light and within a minimum of actual man-power, (guards remain invisible, and may be absent) the panopticon—whether to be used as prison, school army barracks or psychiatric institution— is the diagram of a mechanism of power reduced to an ideal form. Its major effect, Foucault states, is "to automatic functioning power". (Foucault, 1977, p. 201). Its reliance on and exploitation of visibility makes the panopticon more powerful than the darkest dungeon: constant visual control results in subjection and usefulness; in perfect discipline.

Though Foucault himself never made the transition between the panopticon and the male gaze it is evident that his discussion of the panopticon is extremely relevant to gaze theory since it demonstrates in detail the nature of the relation between power and visibility. The panopticon, in fact, may be taken as the perfect metaphor for the gaze; the mechanism that disindividualizes power ... a machinery that assures dissymmetry, disequilibrium, and difference. Foucault focuses on the gaze of the individual physician as the examination of the patient goes on. The physician's gaze symbolically represents the institutional gaze of medicine as it monitors and regulates the bodies of the members of society. The gaze, the focused attention, inscribes the body with meaning and renders it manageable. Together they constitute the docile body 'which may be subjected, used, transformed and improved' (Foucault, 1977, p. 136). Moreover, Foucault also distinguishes what is in my view the most insidious effect of the gaze, that of internalisation. According to him, "He who is subjected to a field of visibility, and who knows it, assumes responsibility for the constraints of power; he makes them play simultaneously upon himself; he inscribes in himself the power relation in which he simultaneously plays both roles; he becomes the principle of his own subjection". (Ibid, pp. 202-203). Consequently, as Shildrick and Price (1996) indicate, "The gaze now cast over the subject body is that of subject herself. What is demanded of her is that she should police her own body, and report in intricate detail its failure to standards of normalcy; that she should render herself in effect transparent At the same time capillary process of power reach deeper into the body, multiplying the norms of function/dysfunction" (Shildrick and Price, 1996, p. 100).

As Jacques Lacan, though from a different perspective, puts it, "We are beings who are looked at; the gaze circumscribes us, and which in the first instance make us beings who are looked at". (Lacan, 1977, p. 72). The gaze, in Lacan's theory, is multiple, 'issuing from all sides'. It is powerful and omnipresent. Also, Lacan speaks of the pre-existence of gaze, "I see only from one point, but in my existence I am looked at from all sides. Thus, the gaze is external ...." (Ibid, p. 74). The external gaze, then, is elusive, 'unapprehensible', a controlling influence that subjects and subjectivates, "the subject tried to adapt himself to it, he becomes that puntiform object ...." Thus, the gaze is most powerful, we may again conclude, when it is internalised" (Lacan, 1977, p. 83).

The relation between visibility and power, between the activity of looking and the use of control is a vital aspect of the characterisation of disability. Throughout their lives, the disabled are constantly watched; the gaze, is always on the alert, omnipresent, differentiating them from the other people, branding them as inferior, the 'cripple', the 'blind', and so on. For what is clearly acknowledged in every theory is that, every gaze is always operative, in a asymmetrical, imbalanced power structure. Though these, undoubtedly are the central aspects of the gaze theory, which postulate the gaze as a socio-cultural regime that subjects and controls women, and is perfected when internalised, another aspect which flows from the notion of gaze is the "stare".

A great deal of thoughtful work by Indian feminists analyses the impact of the evaluative male gaze. However, as I write elsewhere while understanding the nuances of the gaze is indeed significant, another feature of the disabled lives, especially women, is that of encountering the 'stare' (Ghai, 2002c, p. 55). If the male gaze makes normal women appear like passive objects, the stare turns the disabled object into a grotesque sight. Disabled women contend not only with how men look at women but also with how an entire society stares at disabled people, stripping them of any semblance of resistance. 'Public stripping' is a resultant of this gaze and stare, thus leaving the receivers in a state of humiliation and exposure, highlighting their vulnerability in a very intense way. The gaze/stare thus exercises a disciplining power, leaving the disabled people with experiences of shame and invalidation. Neither Indian feminism nor the Indian disability movement acknowledges that disabled women are doubly pinned by a dominant male gaze coupled with the gaze of the culture, which constructs them as objects to be stared at. The stare is an intensified gaze, which constructs the body as deviant and is instrumental in creating an oppressive relationship. As Michael Lenney and Howard Sercombe write, "The interpretation of a look as a stare is clearly contextual and cultural, but in general the risk of staring occurs with any prolonged or fixed gaze on another person especially a stranger" (Lenney and Sercombe, 2002, p. 8).

The disciplinary effect of the stare is internalisation which for women means an estranging influence of their sense of selfhood. The able bodied look at disabled, the disabled watch themselves being looked at; this determines not only most relations between the non-disabled and disabled but also the relation of the disabled to themselves. The surveyor of the disabled in themselves are non-disabled; the surveyed disabled. As John Berger (1975) puts it, in the context of women "Thus she turns herself into an object—and most particularly an object of vision: a sight" (Berger, 1975, p. 47). Disabled women act out of this internalised stare; that as disabled women they are passive and vulnerable. 'Bearer of the Look', identified by what Berger calls her 'to-be-looked-at-ness'. I do not mean to suggest that disabled women cannot resist this stare, but to emphasise the potency of the impact of the internalisation that is situated in a dialectics of power, dominated by the non-disabled's gaze/stare.

Throughout the disability discourse, it has been accepted that one of the greatest difficulties of the disabled is that once they step out, they would be openly stared at, thereby facing an intrusion and invasion of their privacy. Further staring adds on to a perpetuation of stereotypes and myths that associate disability with negativity while it is true that any kind of difference invites stares. However, as Irving Goffman argues, "People with difficulties tend to see staring as an invasion of their privacy and as a negative reaction that implies hostility (Goffman, 1963). In such a context it is not only the physical difference that becomes restrictive, but the "knowledge that each entry into the public world will be dominated by stares, by condescension, by pity and by hostility" (Morris, 1991, p. 25).

The resounding awareness of being stared at and the experience of de-humanisation inherent can only be subverted, if sensitive discourses such as feminism highlight and understand that the identification of disabled women with stigma attached to their disabilities lose out on a sense of agency. As I affirm elsewhere, "Carrying a sense of shame, most [disabled women] find that their voices are silenced as they are always looked upon as the 'Other'. This creates an erosion of agency, thus creating a situation where the disabled woman is not accorded control either on her own life, or that of the dominant group" (Ghai, 2002b, p. 95).

Similarly, Anna Marie Smith (1995) argues, "Hegemony does not take the form of brute domination; it entails instead the delimitations of the intelligible . . . . To fail to achieve an adequate fit within an officially recognised position is to be de-authorised—to be denied recognition as an author of the text and to have one's text dismissed from the start as incoherent, illegitimate or unbelievable"(Smith, 1995, p. 169).

However, this is not to say that there are no disabled women who are resisting this hegemony. As Vatsala an activist puts it, "So big deal, if they stare at me, I stare back at them I tell them in no uncertain terms to mind their own business. And sometimes, I find people who actually want to know something about my disability, not in a derogatory way, but with the intention of coming closer to me. I do explain everything and make them comfortable" (Personal Communication).

Such instances are indicative of the fact that sometimes-negative reactions arise out of an inability to understand the way of reacting to difference. Though many women including the disabled are, sidelined by aesthetics, which aims at operations such as slimming, keeping fit, the proliferation of the slimming and enhanced advertising of fair and lovely creams along with an assortment of beauty tips however, are obviously directed at 'complete' bodies. Yet it is clear that most of us are compared to an inaccessible body ideal. To quote Shildrick and Price further, "The reiteration of the technologies of power speak to a body that remains always in a state of pre-resolution whose boundaries are never secured. Indeed, repetition indicates its own necessary failure to establish any stable body, let alone an ideal one. In the phallocentric order, the female body, whether disabled or not, can never fully answer to the discursive requirements of femininity but remain caught in an endless cycle of body fetishization. In other words, it is a body that always exceeds control" (Shildrick and Price, 1996, p. 105). However control is not possible in case of disabled women, for the ideas "that I can make my limitations disappear", is a form of myth, which becomes the backbone of an internalised sense of oppression. The body then becomes a source of humiliation, something that needs to be hidden.

However, just as the oppression is internalised, so is the ability to contest and resist the negativity associated with one's life. This is evident in so many instances where disabled athletes subvert expectations by displaying performances which are not possible for non-disabled athletes. This interconnectedness of power and resistance is emphasised by Foucault's belief that "there is no power without potential refusal or revolt" (Foucault,1988b, p. 84). It is not as though there are no pointers towards the fact that disabled bodies are never passive. However, as Tremain (2002) says, "Foucault maintained that the disciplinary apparatus of the state, which puts in place the limits of possible conduct by materialising discursive objects through the repetition of regulatory norms, also by virtue of that repetitive process brings into discourse the very conditions for subverting the apparatus itself" (Tremain, 2002, p. 440). Feminists along with disability theorists have to demonstrate that a naturalized body is construction that begs deconstruction, for it is through a thorough deconstruction, that the instability of fixed categories can be challenged. Deconstruction thus dislodges the understanding of identity as fixed and definite. While challenging the fixity, it also attempts to view the significance of context in which that fixity is being advocated. As Diana Fuss puts it, "Deconstruction dislocates the understanding of identity as self-presence and offers, instead, a view of identity as difference. To the extent that identity always contains the sector of non-identity within it, the subject is always divided and identity is always purchased at the price of exclusion of the Other, the repression or repudiation of non-identity"(Fuss, 1989, pp. 102-103).

While deconstruction can assist in breaking down the binary oppositions, the task does not end there. The idea of TAB's i.e, temporarily able bodied, though intended, as an indicator of the precariousness of human existence, is extremely helpful in destabilizing the binaries of health/ill health, non-disabled/disabled. Thus, the boundaries, which divide us into categories, are tangentially wobbly, such that constant replication is needed to keep them in check. In a similar way as we perform our gendered/disabled/sexed/impaired identities, we also need to perform what is expected of a healthy body, so that it is not tainted with bodily breakdown. The negation of binary thought opens up the realm of continual negotiation, within which it might be possible to work towards a truly inclusive society. However, it will be vital to remember that this is not a one time attempt. It has to be conceptualised as a process so that a analytical stance can be generated. A feminist underpinning of disability thus has the potential to question those norms that fail to fully contain or express their ideal standards.

Closures, whether political or academic, do not pave the way for a world order that is changing every day. As I say this I am reminded of Judith Butler who paints the following scenario: "Imagine the situation that a student of mine reports, that of reading a book and thinking, I cannot ask the questions that are posed here because to ask them is to introduce doubt in my political convictions, and to introduce doubt into my political convictions would lead to the dissolution of those convictions. At such a moment, the fear of thinking, indeed, the fear of the question, becomes a moralized defense of politics, and the work of intellectual life and the work of politics are sundered from one another. Politics becomes that which requires certain anti-intellectualism. To remain unwilling to rethink one's politics on the basis of questions posed is to opt for a dogmatic stand at the cost of both life and thought" (Butler, 1997b, p.162).

My attempt therefore is to initiate an inclusive discourse that would make universal sisterhood a distinct possibility. However I have to admit that when I started writing, I was very clear that the writer is and should be held accountable for what she/he has created, but it did not strike me that within my own psyche, I would be haunted by what I have myself excluded. Despite my own experience of disability, I was constricted, whether I liked it or not, by my class, caste, academic background and above all a location, which did not allow me to own up my disability till a very late age. I am absolutely convinced that disability in India is not a singular marker, as it is embedded within a matrix of poverty, caste politics, class struggles, types of impairments and above all patriarchy.

References

Abberley, P. (1997). "The limits of classical social theory in the analysis and transformation of disablement can this really be the end; to be struck inside of mobile with the Memphis blues again"? In *Disability studies: Past, present and future*, eds. Len Barton and M. Oliver. Leeds: The Disability Press.

Abraham, Taisha. (2002). "The Politics of Patriarchy and *Sathin* Bhanwari's Rape". In *Women and the Politics of Violence* ed. Taisha Abraham New Delhi: Shakti Books.

Amos, V, and Parmar, P. (1984). "Challenging imperial feminism". *Feminist Review* 17: 3-20.

Arendt, Hannah. (1958). *The human condition.* Chicago: University of Chicago Press.

Arora, Aditi, and Ghai, Anita. (1997). Parents of children with cerebral palsy speak out: an exploratory study. Project report submitted in partial fulfillment of the requirement for the Bachelor of Arts (honours) degree in Psychology, University of Delhi.

Baquer, Ali, and Sharma Anjali. (1997). *Disability: Challenge vs responses.* New Delhi: Concerned Action Now.

Barnes, C, and Mercer, G. (eds.). (1996). *Exploring the divide: Illness and disability.* Leeds: The Disability Press.

Barnes, C, Mercer, G, and Shakespeare, T. (1999). *Exploring disability: A sociological introduction.* Cambridge: Polity.

Barnes, Colin. (1992). Qualitative research-valuable or irrelevant. *Disability, Handicap and Society.* 7: 115-124.

Baudrillard, Jean. (1983). *In the shadow of the silent majorities......or the end of the social.* Translated by Paul Foss, Paul Patton and John Johnnston. New York: Semiotext(e).

Benhabib, Seyla. (1993). "From identity politics to social feminism: A plea for the nineties". Paper delivered at the symposium. *Science, reason and modern democracy.* Michigan State University.

Berger, P. (1963). *Invitation to sociology: A humanistic perspective.* New York: Anchor Books.

Berger, J. (1975). *Ways of seeing.* Harmondsworth: Penguin.

References

Berger, Peter, and Thomas Luchmann. (1967). *The social construction of reality.* New York: Doubleday.

Bhasin, Kamla, and Nighat Said Khan. (1986). *Some questions on feminism and its relevance in South Asia.* New Delhi: Kali for Women.

Bhogle, Sudha. (1999). "Gender roles: The construct in the Indian context". In *Culture, socialisation and human development: Theory research and applications in India,* ed. T.S. Saraswathi. New Delhi: Sage.

Bogden, R, and Taylor, S. (1989). *Inside out the social meaning of mental retardation.* Toronto: University of Toronto Press.

Bordo, Susan. (1993). *Unbearable weight: Feminism western culture, and the body.* Berkeley: University of California Press.

Bourdieu, Pierre, and Wacquant, Loic. J.D. (1992). *An invitation to reflexive Sociology.* Cambridge and Oxford: Polity.

Butler, Judith. (1991). "Immitation and gender insubordination". In *Inside/out Lesbian theories, gay theories,* ed. Diana Fuss. New York and London: Routledge.

Butler, Judith. (1992). "Contingent foundations: Feminism and the question of 'postmodernism'". In *feminists theorise the political,* ed. Judith Butler and Joan. W. Scott. London and New York: Routledge.

Butler, Judith. (1990). *Gender trouble: Feminisnm and the subversion of identity.* New York: Routledge.

Butler, Judith. (1993). *Bodies that matter: On the discursive limits of Sex.* New York: Routledge.

Butler, Judith. (1997). *Excitable speech: A politics of the performance.* New York and London: Routledge.

Butler, Judith. (1999). New preface to Gender trouble. 2nd edition. New York: Routledge.

Castelnuovo, S, and Guthrie, S.R. (1998). *Feminism and the female body: Liberating the amazon within boulder.* CO: Lynne Rienner Publishers.

Clare, Eli. (2002). "Stolen bodies, reclaimed bodies: Disability and queerness". *Public Culture,* 13(3): 359-365.

Clare, Eli. (1999). *Exile and pride: Disability, queerness, and liberation.* Cambridge, Mass: South End Press.

Collins, P.H. (1997). "Defining black feminist thought". In *The second wave: Reader in feminist theory.* ed. Linda Nicholson. New York and London: Routledge.

Corker, M. (1998). "Disability discourse in a postmodern world". In *The Disability and Reader.* ed. Tom Shakespeare. London and New York: Cassell.

Corker, M. (1999). "Differences, conflations and foundations: The limits to 'accurate' theoretical representation of disabled people's experience". *Disability and society,* 14(5) : 627-642.

Corker, M. (1999b). "Discriminatory Language, talking disability, and the quite revolution in language change". In Annual conference of the British association for applied Linguistics 17th Sept, University of Edinburgh.

Corker, M. (2001). Sensing disability. *Hypatia.* 16(4) fall: 34-52.

Corker, M, and French, S. (1999). *Disability discourse.* Buckingham: Open University Press.

Corker, M, and Shakespeare, T. (eds.) (2002). *Disability/Postmodernity: Embodying disability theory.* London: Continuum.

Crosby, Christina. (1991). *The ends of history: Victorians and the woman question.* London and New York: Routledge.

Crosby, Christina. (1992). "Dealing with differences". In *Feminists theorise the political,* ed. Judith Butler and Joan. W. Scott. London and New York: Routledge.

Crow, L. (1992). "Renewing the social model of disability". *Coalition* (July): 5-9

Crow, Liz. (1996). "Including all of our lives: Renewing the social model of disability". In *Encounters with strangers: Feminism and disability,* ed. Jenny Morris. London: The Women's Press.

Daly, Mary. (1978). *Gyn/Ecology: The metaethics of radical feminism.* Boston: Beacon Press.

Das, Veena. (1979). "Reflections on the social construction of adulthood". In *Identity and adulthood,* (ed.) Sudhir Kakar. Delhi: Oxford University Press.

Das, Veena. (1991). "Composition of the personal voice: Violence and migration". *Studies in History.* 7(1): 65-77.

Das, Veena, and Addlakha, Renu. (2001). "Disability and domestic citizenship: Voice, gender, and the making of a subject". *Public Culture.* 13(3): 511-531.

Davar, V. Bhargavi. (1999). *Mental health of Indian women: A feminist agenda.* New Delhi: Sage.

Davies, C, and Lifchez, R. (1987). "An open letter to architect". In *Rethinking Architecture,* (ed.) R. Lifchez. Berkeley: University of California Press.

Davis, L. J. (1995). *Enforcing normalcy: Deafness, disability and the body.* London: Verso.

Defelice, Robert. (1996). Cited in Mitchell, D. & Synder, S. (1996). "Vital signs: Crip culture talks back". A 48 minute open caption video produced by Brace Yourself Productions, Marquette, Michigan.

de Lauretis, Teresa. (ed.). (1988). F*eminist studies/critical studies.* Houundmills: McMillan.

de Lauretis, Teresa. (1987). *Technologies of gender.* Bloomington: Indiana University Press.

Deleuze, G. (1992). *Foucault.* Minneapolis: University of Minnesota Press.

Descartes, Rene. (1979). *Meditations on the first Philosophy*, translated by Donald A. Indianapolis: Hackett Publishing.

Di Stefafano, Christine. (1990). "Dilemmas of difference: Femininity, modernity and postmodernism". In *Feminism/Postmodernism.* ed. Linda Nicholson. New York and London: Routledge.

Dibernard, B. (1996). "Teaching what I am not: An able bodied woman teaches literature by women with disabilities". In *Teaching what you are not: Identity politics in higher education,* ed. K. Mayberry. New York: New York University Press.

Doniger, W, and B.K. Smith. (1991). *The laws of Manu.* New Delhi: Penguin.

Douglas, Mary. (1975). *Implicit meanings essays in Anthropology.* London: Routledge and Kegan Paul.

Dube, L. (1986). "Seed and earth". In *Visibility and power: Essays on women in society and development,* ed. L. Dube. Delhi: Oxford University Press.

Dyer (2001) cited in Titchkosky, Tanya. (2001). "Disability: A rose by any other name"? The Canadian. *Review of Sociology and Anthropology,* 38(20): 125-140.

Elam, Diane. (1994). *Feminism and deconstruction: Ms. en abyme.* London: Routledge.

Ellison, R. (1952). *Invisible man.* New York: Modern Library.

Epstein, Julia. (1995). *Altered conditions: Disease, medicine and story telling.* London: Routledge.

Erevelles, Nirmala. (2000). "Educating unruly bodies: Critical pedagogy, disability studies and the politics of schooling". *Educational theory.* 50 (1): 25–47.

Erevelles, Nirmala. (2002). "(Im) Material Citizens: Cognitive disability, race, and the politics of citizenship". *Disability, Culture & Education.* 1: 5-25.

Fine, Michele, and Asch, Adrienne. (eds.). (1988). *Women with disabilities: Essays in psychology, culture, and politics.* Philadelphia, PA: Temple University Press.

Finkelstein, V. (1980). *Attitudes and disabled people: Issues for discussion.* New York: World Rehabilitation Fund.

Finkelstein, V. (1996). "Outside inside out". *Coalition* (April): 30-36.

Flax, Jane. (1987). "Postmodernism and gender relations in feminist theory". *Signs.* 12(4): 640.

Foucault, M. (1977). *Discipline and punish: The birth of a the prison,* translated by A. Sheridan. New York: Pantheon Books.

Foucault, M. (1988a). "Technologies of the self". In *Technologies of the self— a seminar with Michel Foucault,* ed. L. H. Martin, H. Gutman & P. H. Hutton. London: Tavistock.

Foucault, M. (1988b). "Power and sex". In *Politics Philosophy Culture: Interviews and other writings*, ed. Lawrence D. Kritzman. London: Routledge.

Frank, A.W. (1995). *The wounded storyteller: Body, illness & ethics*. Chicago. IL: University of Chicago Press.

French, Sally. (1993). "Disability, impairment or something in between". In *disabling barriers, enabling environment*s, ed. John Swain, Vic finkelstein, Sally French, and M. Oliver. London: Sage.

Fuss, Diana. (1989). *Essentially speaking: Feminism, nature and difference*. London: Routledge.

Gable, Susan. (1998). "A theory of an aesthetic on disability". Ann arbor, MII, UMI, dissertation services.

Gallagher, J. Deborah. (2001). "Neutrality as a moral standpoint, conceptual confusion and the full inclusion debate". *Disability & Society* 16(5): 37–655.

Gandhi, Nandita, and Nandita Shah. (1992). *The issues at stake: Theory and practice in the contemporary movement in India*. New Delhi: Kali for women.

Gare, A. (1996). *Nihilism*. Inc. Como, Eco-Logical.

Gatens, Moira. (1990). *Corporeal representations in/and the body politic*. In *Cartographies*, eds. R. Diprose and R. Ferrall. St Leonards: Allen and Unwin.

Gergen, K. J. (1985). "The social constructionist movement in modern Psychology". *American psychologist*. 40 : 266-275.

Gergen, K. (1995). "Social construction and the transformation of identity politics", a draft paper for New Social Science Research symposium, April 7th.

Gergen, K. J. (1990). "Therapeutic professions and the diffusion of deficit". *Journal of Mind and Behavior.* 11: 353-68.

Gergen, K. J., Hoffman, L. and Anderson, H. (1996). "Is diagnosis a disaster? A constructionist trialogue". In *Relational diagnosis*, ed. F. Kaslow. New York: Wiley.

Ghai, Anita. (1998). "Living in the shadow of my disability". *The Journal.* 2 (1): 32–36.

Ghai, Anita. (2000). "Towards understanding disability". *Psychological Studies*. 45(3): 145-149.

Ghai, A. (2001a). "Marginalisation and disability: Experiences from the third world". In *Disability and the life course: Global Perspectives*, ed. Mark. Priestley. Cambridge University Press.

Ghai, A. (2001b). "Human genomics and disability". *Proceedings of the Asian seminar–workshop on new technologies and communities: What next/ where to?* Organized by Community Biodiversity Conservation and Development.

References

Ghai, Anita. (2002a). "Disability in the Indian Context: Post-colonial perspectives". In *Disability and postmodernity: Embodying disability theory*, ed. Mairian Corker, and Tom Shakespeare. London and New York: Continuum.

Ghai, Anita. (2002b). "How Indian mythology portrays disability". *Kaleidoscope* Summer/fall (45): 6-10.

Ghai, Anita. (2002c). "Disabled women: An excluded agenda of Indian feminism" *Hypatia,* 16(4) fall: 34-52.

Goffman, E. (1963). *Stigma:* Notes on *The management of spoiled identity.* Englewood Cliffs, NJ: Prentice Hall.

Goodley, D. (2001). "Learning difficulties, the social model and impairment", *Disability & Society.* 16(2) : 207-231.

Graham, Hilary. (1993). "Social divisions in caring". *Women's Studies International Forum.* 16(5): 461-470.

Grosz, Elizabeth. (1994). *Volatile Bodies: Towards a corporeal feminism.* St. Leonards: Allen and Unwin.

Hahn, H. (1988). "The politics of physical difference: Disability and discrimination", *Journal of Social Issues.* 44 : 39-47.

Hahn, H. (1997). Cited in Thomson, R.G. (1997). *Extraordinary bodies: Figuring physical disability in American culture and literature.* New York: Columbia University Press.

Hall, Stuart. (1994). Cited in Elam, Diane. (1994). *Feminism and deconstruction: Ms. en abyme.* London and New York: Routledge.

Haraway, Donna. (1988). "Situated knowledges: The science question in feminism and the privilege of partial perspective". *Feminist Studies.* 14: 575–99.

Haraway, Donna. (1991). *Simians, cyborgs, and women: The reinvention of nature.* London: Routledge.

Harstock, M, and Nancy, C. (1983). "The feminist standpoint: Developing the ground for a specifically feminist historical materialism". In *Feminist thought discovering reality: Feminist perspectives on epistemology, methodolgy and Philosophy of science.* eds. Sandra Harding and Merill B. Hintikka. Boston: D. Reidel.

Hartsock, Nancy. (1990). "Foucault on power: A theory for women"? In *Feminism/postmodernism.* ed. Linda Nicholson. New York and London: Routledge.

Hedlund, Marianne. (2000). "Disability as a phenomena: A discourse of social and biological understanding", *Disability Society.* 15 (50): 765-780.

Hendy, N, and Pascal, G. (1998). "Independent living: Gender, violence and the threat of violence". *Disability & Society.* 13 (3): 415-427.

Hillyer, Barbara. (1993). *Feminism & disability*. Norman and London: University of Oklahoma Press.
hooks, bell. (1984). *Feminist theory: From margin to center*. Boston: South End Press.
hooks, bell. (1990). *Yearning: Race, gender and cultural politics*. Boston: South End Press.
Hughes, B, and Paterson, K. (1997). "The social model of disability and the disappearing body: Towards a sociology of impairment". *Disability & Society*. 12 (3): 325-40.
Hughes, B. (1999). "The constitution of impairment: Modernity and the aesthetic of oppression". *Disability & Society* 12 : 155-172.
Hughes, B. (2000). "Medicine and the aesthetic invalidation of disabled people" *Disability & society* 15(4) : 555-568.
IFSHA. (1999). "A conference on women and sexual abuse". (Intervention for support, healing and awareness): 'C52, 2nd Floor, South Extension, part II, New Delhi, India. 68.
International Classification of Impairment, Disability, and Handicap (ICIDH). 1980. Geneva: World Health Organisation.
Israel, P, and Mcpherson, C. (1983). Introduction. In *Voices from the shadow: Women with disabilities speak out*. ed. G. F. Matthews. Toronto Ontario: The Women's Educational Press.
Jenkins, R. (1996). *Social Identity*. London: Routledge.
Johri, Rachana. (1998). "Cultural constructions of maternal attachment: The case of a girl child" Ph.D. diss., University of Delhi, India.
Kakar, Sudhir, and Chowdhary, K. (1970). *Conflict and choice: Indian youth in a changing society*. Bombay: Somaiya.
Kakar, Sudhir. (1978). *The inner world: A psychoanalytic study of childhood and society in India*. Delhi: Oxford University Press.
Kapadia, Shagufa. (1999). "Self, women and empowerment: A conceptual inquiry". In *Culture, socialisation and human Development: Theory research and applications in India*. ed. T.S. Saraswathi. New Delhi: Sage.
Keller, Helen. (1924). As cited in Crow, Liz. (2000). Helen Keller: Rethinking the problematic icon. *Disability & Society.* 15(6): 845-860.
Kriegel, L. (1982). "The wolf in the pit in the zoo". *Social Policy (*fall):16-23.
Krishnaji, N. (2000). "Trends in sex ratio". *Economic and political weekly* (April): 1161–1163.
Lacan, J. (1977). *The four fundamental concepts of Psychoanalysis, Jaques-*Aalain Miller (ed.) translated by A. Sheridan. H armondsworth: Penguin. (original French edn 1973).
Lackmund, J. (1998). "Between scrutiny and treatment: Physical diagonosis and the restructuring of 19th century medical practice". *Sociology of Health and Illness*. 20: 779-801.

Lenny Michael, and Howard Sercombe. (2002). "Did you see that guy in the wheelchair down the pub? Interactions across difference in a public place". *Disability & Society.* 17(1) : 5-18.

Liddle, Joanna, and Rai, Shirin M. (1993). "Between feminism and orientalism". In *Making connections: Womem's studies, women's movements, women's lives.* ed. Mary Kennedy, Cathy Lubelska and val Walsh. London: Taylor and Francis.

Linton, Simi. (1998). *Claiming disability: Knowledge and identity.* New York: New York.

Lister, Ruth. (1997). *Citizenship: Feminist perspectives.* Basingstoke: Macmillan.

Llewellyn, A, and Hogan K. (2000). The use and abuse of models of disability *Disability & Society.* 15(1): 157-165.

Lonsdale, Susan. (1990). *Women and disability: The experience of physical disability among women.* Basingstoke: MacMillan Press.

Lorde, Audre. (1981). "The master's tools will never dismantle the master's house". In *This bridge called my back: Writings by radical women of color.* ed. Cherrie Moraga and Gloria Anzaldua. New York: Kitchen Table Press.

Mangala, Charu, and Ghai, Anita. (2000). "Understanding motherhood in the context of a developmentally disabled girl child: An exploratory study". Project report submitted in partial fulfillment of the requirement for the Bachelor of Arts(honours) degree in Psychology, University of Delhi.

Mairs, N. (1996). *Carnal acts.* Boston, MA: Beacon Press.

Martin, L, Gutman, H, and Hutton P. (eds.). (1988). *Technologies of the self.* London: Tavistock.

Mason, M. (1992). "A nineteen-parent family". In *Alone together: Voices of single mothers.* ed. J. Morris. London: The women's Press.

Mason, Micheline, cited in Campbell, J. and Oliver, M. (1996), (eds.). *Disability politics.* London: Routledge.

Mead Cited in Anthias and Kelly. (1995). *Sociological debates: Thinking about the* social. Dartford: Greenwitch University Press.

Meaghan, Morris. Cited in Kwok, Wei Leng (1995). "New Australian feminism: Towards a discursive politics of Australian feminist thought". *Antithesis* 7(1): 47 –63.

Meekosha, Helen. (1990). *Is feminism ablebodied? Reflections from between the trenches.* Refractory Girl (August): 34-42

Meekosha, Helen. (1998). "Body battles: Bodies gender and disability". In *The disability reader,* ed. Tom Shakespeare. London and New York: Cassell.

Meekosha, Helen. (2000). "A disabled genius in the family: Personal musings on the tale of two sisters". *Disability & Society.* 15(5): 811-15.

Mehra, Preeti. (2000). "Women with disabilities: Lost opportunities and fresh hopes". In *Diary of the dispossessed,* eds. S. Venkatesh and Sunita Bhadauria. Banglore: Books for Change.

Memmi, Albert. (1967). *The colonizer and the colonized*. Boston: Beacon Press.

Menon, Nivedita. (2002c). Cited in Ghai Anita (2002c). "Disabled women: An excluded agenda of Indian feminism". *Hypatia*. 16(4) : 1-16.

Menon, Nivedita. (1996). "The impossibility of 'justice': Female foeticide and feminist discourse on abortion". In *Social reform, sexuality and the state*. ed. Patricia Uberoi. New Delhi: Sage.

Michalko, Rod. (1998a). "The mystery of the eye and the shadow of blindness". Toronto: University of Toronto Press.

Ministry of Women and Child Welfare. Policy document on empowerment of women, (2000), Government of India, India.

Mitchell, W. J. T. (2001). "Seeing disability. *Public Culture*. 13(3): 391-397.

Mohanty, Chandra. (1988). Under Western eyes: Feminist scholarship and colonial discourse". *Feminist Review*. 30: 61-88.

Morris, J. (1991). *Pride and Prejudice: Transforming attitudes to disability*. London: The Women's Press.

Morris, Jenny. (1993a). "Feminism and disability". *The Feminist Review*. 43 (Spring): 57-70.

Morris, Jenny. (1993b). "Gender and disability". In *disabling barriers, enabling environments*. eds. John Swain, Vic finkelstein, Sally French, and M. Oliver. London: Sage.

Morris, Jenny. (ed.) (1996). *Encounters with strangers: Feminism and disability*. London: The Women's Press.

Morris, Jenny. (2001). "Impairment and disability: constructing an ethics of care that promotes human rights". *Hypatia*. 16(4) : 1-16.

Mouffe, C. (1992). "Feminism, citizenship, and radical democratic politics". In *Feminists theorise the political*. ed. Judith Butler and Joan W. Scott. London and New York: Routledge.

Nicholson, L. (1998). *Feminism/Postmodernism:* Routledge.

Nicholson, Linda. (1994). "Interpreting gender". *Signs: Journal of Women in Culture and Society*. 20 (11) : 79-105.

Nicholson, Linda. (1995). "Interpreting gender". In *Social postmodernism*. eds. Steven Seidman and Linda Nicholson. Cambridge: Cambridge University Press.

Niranjana, Seemanthini. (2001). *Gender and space: Femininity, sexualisation and the female body*. New Delhi: Sage.

Niranjana, Seemanthini. (1998). "Femininity, space and the female body: An anthropological perspective". In *Embodiment: Essays on gender and identity*. ed. M. Thapan. New Delhi: Oxford University Press.

Oliver, M. and Barnes, C. (1998). *Social policy and disabled people: From exclusion to inclusion*. London: Longman.

Oliver, M. (1983). *Social work with disabled people*. Basingstoke: MacMillan.
Oliver, M. (1990). *The politics of disablement*. Basingstoke: MacMillan.
Oliver, M. (1996a). *Understanding disability: From theory to practice*. London: MacMillan.
Oliver, M. (1996b). "Defining impairment and disability". In *Exploring the divide: Illness and disability*. ed. Colin Barnes and Michael Oliver. Leeds: Disability Press.
Oliver, M. and Sapey, B. (1999). *Social work with disabled people*, 2nd edn. Basingstoke: Macmillan.
Papanek, H. (1990). "To each less than she needs, from more than she can do: Allocations, entitlements and value". In *Persistent inequalities: Women and world development*. ed. Tinker. New York: Oxford University Press.
Parmar, Pratibha. (1990). *Black feminism: The politics of articulation identity: Community, culture and difference*. ed. Jonathan Rutherford. London: Lawrence and Wishart.
Peters, S. (2000). "Is there a disability culture? A syncretisation of three possible world views". *Disability & Society*. 15(4): 583-602.
Price, Janet, and Margrit Shildrick (1998). "Uncertain thoughts on the dis/abled body". In *Vital signs: Feminist reconfigurations of the bio/logical body*. ed. Margrit Shildrick and Janet Price. Edinburgh: Edinburgh University Press.
Price, Janet, and Margrit Shildrick (2002). "Bodies together: Touch, ethics and disability". In *Disability and postmodernity: Embodying disability theory*. (ed.) Mairiaw Corker and Tom Shakespeare. London and New York: Continuum.
Priestley, Mark. (1998). "Constructions and creations: Idealism, materialism and disability theory". *Disability & Society*, 13, 75-94.
Priestley, Mark. (2001). (ed.). *Disability and the life course: Global perspectives*. Cambridge University Press.
Rao, S. K. R. (1969). *Social institutions among the Hindus*. Mysore: Rao and Raghav.
Rao, Shridevi. (2001). "A little inconvenience: Perspectives of Bengali families of children with disabilities on labelling and inclusion". *Disability & Society*. 16(4): 531-548.
Rich, A. (1976). *Of woman born: Motherhood as experience and institution*. New York: Norton.
Riley, Denise. (1988). *Am I that name? Feminism and the category of women in history*. Minneapolis: University of Minnesota Press.
Roof, J. and Wiegman, R. (eds.). (1995). "Who can speak? Authority and critical identity". Chicago IL: University of Illinois Press.

Rose, Jacqueline. (1985). "Introduction II Feminine sexuality: Jacques Lacan and the ecole freudienne", eds. Juliet Mitchell and Jacquaeline Rose. New York: Norton.
Rose, N. (1996). "Authority and genealogy of subjectivity". In *Detraditionalisation.* eds. P. Heels, S. Lash and P. Morris. Oxford: Blackwell.
Rutherford, J. (1990). *Identity: Community, culture, difference.* London: Lawrence and Wishart.
Sadgopal, A. (2000). *Shiksha ka sawal.* India: Granth Shilpi India Pvt. Ltd.
Said, Edward. (1978). *Orientalism.* New York: Pantheon.
Sampson, Edward. (1993). *Celebrating the other: A dialogic account of human nature.* London: Harvester Wheatsheaf.
Schriempf, Alexa. (2001). "(Re)fusing the amputated body: An interactionist bridge for feminism and disability". *Hpatia: A journal of feminist philosophy.* 16 (4): 53-79.
Scott, Joan. (1992). "Experience". In *Feminists theorise the political,* eds. Judith Butler and Joan. W. Scott. London and New York: Routledge.
Scott, Wallach Joan. (1988). *Gender and the politics of history.* New York: Columbia University Press.
Sen, Anima. (1988). *Psychosocial integration of the handicapped: A challenge to the society.* Delhi: Mittal Publications.
Seymour, W. (1998). *Remaking the body: Rehabilitation and change.* London and New York: Routledge.
Shakespeare, T. (1997). "Cultural representations of disabled people: Dustbins for disavowal". In *Disability studies: Past, present and future.* eds. L. Barton and M. Oliver. 217-236. Leeds: Disability Press.
Shakespeare, T. W. (1992). "A reply to Liz crow" *Coalition* (September) 40.
Shakespeare, T. W., and Watson, N. (1997). "Defending the social model", *Disability & Society.* 12(2) : 293-300.
Shariff, Abusaleh. (1999). *India: Human development report: A profile of Indian states in the 1990s.* London: Oxford University Press.
Sharma, N. (1996). *Identity of the adolescent girl.* New Delhi: Discovery publishing.
Shildrick, Margrit, and Price Janet. (1996). "Breaking the boundaries of the broken body". *Body and Society.* 2(4) : 1-15.
Silvers, A. (1998). "Review of deaf and disabled or deafness disabled". *Deaf worlds.* 14(3): 31-32.
Smith, A. M. (1995). "The regulation of lesbian sexuality through erasure: The case of Jennifer Saunders". In *Lesbian Erotics.* (ed) Karla Jay. New York: New York University Press.
Sontag, S. (1979). *Illness as a metaphor.* New York: Vintage.

References

Spivak, G. C. (1988). "Can the subaltern speak"? In *Marxism and the interpretation of culture. (ed.)* C. Nelson and L. Grossberg. Urbana, IL: University of Illinois Press.

Spivak, G. C. (1990). "The Post-Colonial critic: Interviews, strategies, dialogues", (ed.) Sarah Harasym. London: Routledge.

Srinivas, M. N. (1978). *The changing position of Indian women.* Delhi: Oxford University Press.

Stone, Emma (ed.). (1999). *Disability and development.* The Disability Press: Leeds.

Sutcliffe, J., and Simons, K. (1993). *Self advocacy with people with learning disabilities.* Leicester, NIACE.

Swain, J, and French, Sally. (2000). "Towards an affirmative model of disability" *Disability & Society.* 15(4) : 569-582.

Synnott, A. (1993). *The Body social: Symbolism, self and society.* London: Routledge.

Thapan, Meenakshi. (1998). *Embodiment: Essays on gender and identity.* New Delhi: Oxford University Press.

Thomas, Carol. (1999). *Female Forms.* Buckingham: Open University Press.

Thomson, R.G. (1997). *Extraordinary Bodies: Figuring Physical disability in American culture and literature.* New York: Columbia University Press.

Titchkosky, Tanya. (2001). "Disability: A rose by any other name? The Canadian Tanya Titchkosky". *Review of Sociology and Anthropology,* 38 (20) : 125-140.

Tremain, Shelley. (2000). Review of *Female Forms.* Buckingham: Open University Press. *Disability & Society.* 15(5) : 825-829.

Tremain, Shelley. (2002). "On the subject of impairment". In *Disability and postmodernity: Embodying disability theory.* (ed.) M. Corker, and Tom Shakespeare. London and New York: Continuum

Trinh, Minh-ha. (1989). *Woman, native, Other.* Bloomington: Indiana University Press.

Tuana, Nancy. (1996). "Fleshing gender, sexing the body: Refiguring the sex gender distinction". *The Southern Journal of Philosophy: Rethinking sex and gender.* 35 supplement.

Tuana, Nancy. (2001). "Material locations: An interactionalist alternative to realism/social constructivism". In *Engendering rationalities,* (ed.) Sandra Morgen and Nancy Tuana. New York: SUNY Press.

UPIAS (1976). "The Fundamental Principles of Disability". London: UPIAS.

Vernon, A. (1999). "The dialectics of multiple identities and the disabled people's movement", *Disability & Society,* 14 : 167-173.

Wade, Cheryl Marie. (1994). "Identity". *The disability rag and resource* (September/October) 32-36.

Weed, Elizabeth. (1989). *Introduction: Terms of reference. Coming to terms.* New York and London: Routledge.

Welsch, W. (1996). "Aestheticization processes: Phenomena, distinctions and prospects". *Theory, Culture and Society*, 13(1) : 1-24.

Wendell, Susan. (1997). "Towards a feminist theory of disability". In *The Disability Studies Reader*. ed. I. L. Davis London: Routledge.

Wendell, Susan (2001). "Unhealthy disabled: Treating chronic illness as disabilities". *Hypatia*. 16(4) : 17-33.

Wendell, Susan. (1996). *The rejected body: Feminist Philosophical reflections on disability.* New York: Routledge.

White, H. (1978). *Tropics of discourse.* New York: John Hopkins University Press.

William, Gareth. (1996). "Representing disability: Some questions of phenemenology and politics". In *Exploring the divide: Illness and disability,* eds. C. Barnes, C. and G. Mercer. Leeds: The Disability Press.

Winnicot, D. W. (1965). *The Maturational processes and the facilitating environment.* London: Hogarth Press.

Young, I. M. (1990). *Justice and the politics of difference.* Princeton, NJ: Princeton University Press.

Young, Robert. Forthcoming. "Invisibility and blue eyes: Towards a theory of African American subjectivity". *Revista Canaria de estudios Ingless*.

Younkin, L. (1989). Crips on parade. *Disability Rag*. 30-33.

Zola, Irving Kenneth. (1982). *Missing pieces: A chronicle of living with a disability.* Philadelphia, PA, Temple University Press.

Zola, I. (1991). "Bringing our bodies and ourselves back in: Reflections on a past, present and future medical sociology". *Journal of health and social behaviour*. 32 : 1-16.

Zola, I. (1998). Cited in Meekosha, Helen (1998). "Body battles: Bodies, gender and disability". In *The disability reader.* ed. Tom Shakespeare. London and New York: Cassell.

Index

Abberley, P. 119
Able-bodied society 37, 44
Abraham, T. 32
Addlakha, R. 65
Alterity 79
Amos, V. 81
Arendt, H. 145
Aristotle 105
Arora, A. 74, 155
Asch, A. 18, 71, 125
Ashtvakra, 47

Barnes, C. 28, 29, 35, 43
Baudrillard, J. 149
Bentham 157
Berger, J. 160
Berger, P. 45
Better dead than disabled approach 69
Bhanwari Devi, 32
Bhasin, K. 89
Bhogle, S. 58
Biological body 114
    foundationalism 125, 128, 130
    impairment 88
Black feminist movement 139
Bogden, Robert 46
Bordo, S. 114
Bourdieu, W. 113
Brown, P. 46
Butler, J. 84, 125, 126, 127, 143, 163

Cartesian divide of mind and body 114
Caste 50, 152
Castelnuovo, S. 73
Census of 1991 33
    2001 33, 69
Chodorow, N. 84
Chowdhary, K. 66
Clare, E. 132, 147
Class 49, 50, 152

Collins, P. H. 139, 140
Corker, M. 32, 48, 49, 51, 92, 106, 107, 108, 109, 110, 111, 136, 142
Crosby, C. 85, 86, 144
Crow, L. 44, 51, 120, 122, 123, 129, 138

Dalit 137
Daly, M. 81
Das, V. 58, 65, 114
Davar, B. 77, 78, 155, 156
Davies, C. 153
Davis, L. 116, 117
de, Lauretis T. 125, 157
Deconstruction 83, 154, 162
DeFelice, R. 55
Descartes, R. 116
Dibernard, B. 149, 150
Dichotomisation 125
    impairment and disability 125
    sex and gender 127
    nature and nurture 127
Difference 57, 95, 139, 148
Difficult childhood 57
Disability, definitions of 28, 29
    legislation 56
    movement 51, 92
    status 50
Disabled body 114
    children 58, 74, 91-112
    feminists 120
    girl child 58, 59
    identity 108, 134
    people's movement 92, 93
Disease/disability/impairment 30
Doniger, W. 62
Double disadvantage 93
    oppression 92, 113, 117
Douglas, M. 115
Dube, L. 64, 65
Dyer 54

Education 60, 61
Elam, D. 85, 123, 124, 127
Ellison, R. 39
   Invisible Man 39
Epstein, J. 142
Erevelles, N. 126
Essentialism 48, 108
Exclusion 83, 87

Female Forms 101
Feminist discourse 91-112, 113, 114
   movement 83
Fine, M. 71, 125
Finkelstein, V. 42, 118
Foucauldian exercises in disciplinary power 32
Foucault, M. 130, 131, 157, 158, 162
   Discipline and Punish 157
French, S. 38, 51, 110, 133, 134
Fuss, D. 162

Gallagher, D. 46
Gandhi, N. 87
Gare, A. 151
Gaze 151, 157, 158, 159
Gatens, M. 13
Gender 49, 50, 51, 103, 105, 117, 123, 124, 125, 126, 130, 149, 152
Gergen, K. 29, 53, 134
Ghai, A. 44, 47, 48, 50, 52, 58, 60, 70, 72, 73, 74, 77, 136, 155, 159, 160
Gillgan, C. 84
Girl child 58
Goffman, I. 160
Goodley, D. 121
Graham, H. 154
Grosz, E. 99, 127
   Volatile Bodies 99
Gujrat 33
Guthrie, S.R. 73

Hahn, H. 41, 72
Hall, S. 142
Handicap 30
Haraway, D. 109, 149
   Situated Knowledge 109
Harstock, N. 82, 84, 140

Healthy disabled 121
Hendy, N. 156, 157
Heumann, J. 105
Hillyer, B. 74, 100, 156
   Discipline and Feminism 100
Hogan, K. 28
hooks, b. 108
Hughes, B. 79, 119, 122, 152
Hyper-visible 39

Identity 106
Identity politics 132, 134
IFSHA: A report on women violence and mental health 77
Impairment 30, 42, 49, 120, 122, 123, 154,
   and sex 117
   versus disability 114
Individual materialist models 45
   /medical model of disability 34
Individualist idealist model 45
Intelligence Quotient (IQ) 36
International classification of impairments 30
Issues of (A)Sexuality 71
IYDP (International Year of Disabled People) 17

Jenkins, R. 146
Johar, R. 66
Johri, R. 58, 62
Jouissance 116

Kakar, S. 66, 68
Kanyadan 62
Kapadia, S. 74
Khan, N. S. 19
Kargil 33
Keller, H. 138
Kriegel, L. 34
Krishanji, N. 69

Lacan, J. 151, 157, 158, 159
Lackmund, J. 34
Language 54
   of disability 98
Lenney, M. 159, 160
Liddle, J. 81
Lifchez, R. 153

Index

Linton, S. 35, 33, 134
Lister, R. 140
Llewellyn, A. 28
Lord Shiva 48
Lorde, A. 144
Luckmann, T. 45

Mahabharata 47
Mairs, N. 148
Male-centric approach 51, 57, 92,
    disability movement 113
Mangla, C. 74, 155
Manusmriti 62
Marxian theory 84
Mason, M. 51
Medical model of disability 34
Meekosha, H. 70, 92, 98, 100, 133
Mehra, P. 57
Memmi, A. 79, 80, 81, 83
Menon, N. 69, 90
Mercer, G. 35
Middle class 51, 66
    feminists 103
    women's issues 140
Ministry of Women and Child Welfare 77
Mitchell, W.J.T. 39, 55
Mobius strip 127
Mohanty, C. 81
Mohit, A. 57
Morris, J. 51, 92, 93, 94, 95, 96, 117, 120, 132, 155, 156, 160
    Pride against Prejudice 132
Morris, M. 29
Mother-blaming 75
Mothering a disabled daughter 73
Mothers in India 75
Mouffe, C. 143

National Policy for Empowerment of Women 77
Nicholson, L. 130
Niranjana, S. 61, 78, 114
    Gender and Space 61
Non-disabled 120
    and disabled body 126
    bodies 127
    feminists 93
    people 42, 122
    person 38, 39, 55, 121
    woman 116
    world's reactions 94
    /able-bodied values 153
Normal/abnormal 112
Normalcy 35
Normativism 108
North Indian Punjabi culture 72

Oliver, M. 29, 36, 42, 43, 118, 119, 127, 157
Orientalism 81, 82
Orissa 33
Othering process 79, 83, 88, 120, 142

Papanek, H. 74
Parmar, P. 81, 137
Pascal, G. 156, 157
Paterson, K. 15, 119, 122
Person first approach 55
Personal communications 57, 60, 61, 70, 151, 156, 161
Persons with Disabilities Act (Equal opportunities) 30, 31
Peters, S. 41, 134
Postmodernist approach to disability 48
Price, J. 32, 48, 92, 111, 112, 141, 142 148, 158, 161
Priestley, M. 44, 54
Psychology 36

Quality of life 35

Race 49, 50, 149
Rai, S. 81
Ramayana 47
Rao, S. 55, 64
Reality 110
Rehabilitation 35
Rejected body 95
Relation between power and visibility 158, 159
    gender and culture 124
    mind and body 114
    non-disabled and disabled 132
    spatiality and the quality of disabled women's lives 153

the parents and the disabled children/
    adults 155
  women and men 103
Restrictions of activity 101, 102
Re-thinking disability 146-163
Rich, A. 96
Riley, D. 86
Roof, J. 91
Rose, J. 80, 124
Rutherford, J. 87

Sadgopal, A. 60
Said, E. 26, 81, 82, 83
Sampson, E. 82
Sapey, B. 157
Sati 81
Schriempf, A. 122, 127, 128, 129, 130
Scott, J. 94, 125
  Gender and the Politics of History 94
Self-defeating 118
  identity 150
  perceptions 119
  sufficiency 120, 155
Sensibility 109
Sercombe, H. 159, 160
Sex 123, 126
Sexual identity 124
Sexuality 49
Seymour, W. 119
Shah, N. 87
Shakespeare, T. 80, 81, 118, 119, 133
Shariff, A. 37
Sharma, N. 66
Shildrick, M. 32, 48, 92, 111, 112, 141, 142, 148, 158, 161
Shrivastava, J. 89
Silvers, A. 108, 109
Simons, K. 29
Smith, K 62
Smith, A. M. 161
Social modle of disability 41, 45
Social construction 22, 26, 45, 46, 47, 48, 94, 96, 99, 117, 119, 122, 123, 148
Sontag, S. 33, 34
Spivak, G.C. 142
Srinivas, M.N. 64

Stefano, C. Di 56
Steven T. 46
Stone, E. 107
Surdas 47, 55
Sutcliffe, J. 29
Swain, J. 38, 133, 134
Synder, S. 55
Synnott, A. 152

TAB 38, 162
Terminology 24, 25, 28, 53, 54, 55, 107
Thapan, M. 114
Third world 49
Thomas, C. 92, 101, 102, 133
Thomson, R. G. 92, 103, 104, 105, 106, 133
  Extraordinary Bodies 103
Titchkosky, T. 55
Tragedy model of disability 38
Tremain, S. 102, 130, 131, 162
Trinh, M. ha 124, 143
Tuana, N. 128, 129

Understanding disability 28-55
Union of Physically Impaired Against Segregation (UPIAS) 42, 51, 54, 101, 103, 118
Universalised disability discourse 104, 107

Vernon, A. 136
Viewers Forum on Disability 55

Wade, C. M. 120, 134
Watson, N. 133
Welfare State 100
Welsch, W. 88, 89
Wendell, S. 39, 46, 92, 95, 96, 97, 98, 121, 132, 133, 152
  The Rejected Body 46
Wiegman, R. 91
Women's movement 87, 88
World Health Organisation (WHO) 30, 32

Young, I.M. 39, 138, 155
Younkin, L. 134

Zola, I. 38, 70